E-books

Other Books in the Current Controversies Series

Assisted Suicide

Developing Nations

Espionage and Intelligence

Gasoline

Gays in the Military

Global Warming

Human Trafficking

Importing from China

The Iranian Green Movement

Jobs in America

Medicare

Modern-Day Piracy

Nuclear Armament

Politics and Religion

Rap and Hip Hop

Vaccines

Women in Politics

I E-books

Debra A. Miller, Book Editor

GREENHAVEN PRESS
A part of Gale, Cengage Learning

Detroit • New York • San Francisco • New Haven, Conn • Waterville, Maine • London

Elizabeth Des Chenes, *Director, Publishing Solutions*

© 2013 Greenhaven Press, a part of Gale, Cengage Learning

Gale and Greenhaven Press are registered trademarks used herein under license.

For more information, contact:
Greenhaven Press
27500 Drake Rd.
Farmington Hills, MI 48331-3535
Or you can visit our Internet site at gale.cengage.com

For product information and technology assistance, contact us at

Gale Customer Support, 1-800-877-4253
For permission to use material from this text or product, submit all requests online at www.cengage.com/permissions

Further permissions questions can be emailed to permissionrequest@cengage.com

Articles in Greenhaven Press anthologies are often edited for length to meet page requirements. In addition, original titles of these works are changed to clearly present the main thesis and to explicitly indicate the author's opinion. Every effort is made to ensure that Greenhaven Press accurately reflects the original intent of the authors. Every effort has been made to trace the owners of copyrighted material.

Cover image copyright © Efired/Shutterstock.com.

LIBRARY OF CONGRESS CATALOGING-IN-PUBLICATION DATA

E-books / Debra A. Miller, book editor.
p. cm. -- (Current controversies)
Includes bibliographical references and index.
ISBN 978-0-7377-6223-5 (hardcover) -- ISBN 978-0-7377-6224-2 (pbk.)
1. Electronic books. I. Miller, Debra A.
Z1033.E43E37 2013
070.5'73--dc23

2012033959

Printed in the United States of America
1 2 3 4 5 6 7 17 16 15 14 13

Contents

Foreword   11

Introduction   14

Chapter 1: Are E-books Better than Paper Books?

Chapter Preface   18

Yes: E-books Are Better than Paper Books

E-books Have Many Advantages Compared to Traditional Books   21

Jason Cross and Melissa J. Perenson

E-books offer many benefits. For example, they are paperless, do not take up physical space, resizable, and completely portable.

E-books Have Great Benefits for Academic and Research Libraries   26

Sue Polanka

E-books can be beneficial to academic and research libraries by reducing libraries' storage needs and maintenance costs while giving library users round-the-clock access.

E-books Allow Authors to Self-Publish Easily   32

Bethany Ramos

Authors can self-publish e-books simply and quickly by uploading an edited manuscript onto Amazon, an online book publisher, thereby sharing their writing worldwide without a traditional publishing company.

No: E-books Are Not Better than Paper Books

Paper Books Are Still the Best Way to Read Books   34

Eric Sammons

Paper books are far superior to e-books and will continue to be the favored way to read books. However, e-books are useful for certain types of publications, such as magazines and textbooks.

E-books Will Widen the Digital Divide   38

Christopher Mims

E-books destroy the flexibility and control that readers and libraries have historically had with printed books. E-books require the purchase of an e-reader—something that children in poverty may not be able to afford.

E-books Are Not Greener than   41
Paper Books

Sierra Club Green Home

Whether e-books are more ecological than printed books is debated variously, but this viewpoint concludes that borrowing books from the public library is the best ecological choice.

Chapter 2: Should Libraries Buy and Lend E-books?

Chapter Preface   45

Yes: Libraries Should Buy and Lend E-books

There Should Be a Vibrant Rental   48
of E-books by Libraries

Martin Taylor

Library e-book lending has not taken off, largely because of concerns by publishers and authors. There should be a library rental system for e-books, perhaps with delayed e-book release dates, similar to the film release model, which would keep libraries relevant and compensate authors and publishers fairly.

The E-book Market Must Open to   53
Facilitate E-book Usage by Libraries

Tim Kambitsch

The e-book/library market should be more open. E-book purchases should be separate from the hosting formats of those materials on e-readers, allowing libraries and their patrons more flexibility.

E-book Sellers Should Listen to   59
the Concerns of Libraries

Kate Sheehan

When HarperCollins announced it was limiting library e-book purchases to twenty-six circulations, many librarians boycotted the publisher. The boycott served as a demand for publishers to hear the concerns of libraries for a tiered e-book plan.

Both Libraries and Book Publishers   62
Should Respond Creatively to the Public
Demand for E-books
Kent Anderson
Publishers should not limit the supply of e-books when demand is skyrocketing. E-books are changing the way books are made and sold, and both publishers and libraries should avoid clinging to the past.

No: Libraries Should Not Buy and Lend E-books

Libraries Should Get Out of the   65
E-book Business
Bobbi Newman
Even though about 30 percent of the public wants e-books, libraries should not spend tax money on them right now. The whole e-book market is in flux, so libraries should put their money elsewhere until solutions are found.

There Are Good Reasons for Libraries   69
Not to Use E-books Yet
Evan Williamson
The e-book market is new and still in transition, so libraries should hold off from entering the fray for now.

Many Libraries Cannot Afford   72
E-book Prices
Michael Kelley
When Random House significantly increased its prices for e-books sold to libraries, many librarians protested. Libraries are already facing budget problems, and many librarians agree that the new prices are not affordable.

Chapter 3: How Should E-books Be Priced?

Chapter Preface   78

E-book Pricing Should Be Decided   81
by E-book Publishers

TendersInfo News

Amazon inhibits the free market by meddling in e-book pricing. The publishers should be able to set the pricing of their products. This allows the market to decide what it is willing to pay for e-books.

E-book Consumers Prefer Amazon's   83
Low E-book Prices

Charles Cooper

American e-book consumers thought that e-readers would save them money, but publishers are trying to maintain higher e-book prices by changing the distribution system from a wholesale model to an agency model.

Public Libraries Should Root for Amazon   87
to Win the E-book Pricing War

PublicLibraries.com

Amazon stopped selling e-books published by the Independent Publishers Group, which wanted its e-books sold at a higher price. Public libraries should hope Amazon prevails because it will mean significantly lower e-book prices.

Publishers Must Price E-books Higher   89
than Amazon to Cover Publishing Costs

Curt Matthews

Although e-books have no printing, shipping, or storage costs, they do require editorial and marketing services just like printed books. E-book prices must reflect the true publishing costs.

E-book Publishers May Lose by   93
Keeping E-book Prices Artificially High

Mathew Ingram

Book publishers' fight for the agency model of e-book pricing—in order to keep e-book prices and profit margins high—may be a losing proposition.

Amazon's Predatory Pricing
Could Destroy Bookstores and
Print Book Publishers
96

Husna Haq

The US Department of Justice has proposed an antitrust lawsuit against Apple and five book publishers for using an agency model for e-book pricing that could actually decrease competition. With the wholesale model, Amazon's artificially low e-book prices could destroy bookstores and publishers.

The US Department of Justice
E-book Lawsuit Will Have Little Effect
on Price Competition
99

Matthew Yglesias

The US Department of Justice lawsuit against Apple and book publishers claiming that they colluded to raise e-book prices will not have much impact. The publishing revolution that is being driven by e-books will continue.

Chapter 4: What Is the Future for E-books?

Chapter Preface
105

The Future of Writing Is Digital
107

Sam Harris

Writers and publishers are facing a big problem as a result of the popularity of social media and e-books: readers are increasingly expecting digital writing to be free. The future for writers may be digital, but they must find a way to be paid.

E-books and Paper Books Will
Coexist
114

Jan Swafford

E-books, like every new technology, change the way people perceive and understand. E-books offer different options than print books do, and in the end they will coexist with print books, not replace them.

E-books Are Already Creating
a Self-Publishing Revolution
120

Deirdre Donahue

E-books are dramatically changing the publishing industry, allowing authors to circumvent traditional publishers and self-publish their books online. This self-publishing revolution, however, may not mean the end of traditional book publishers.

Five E-book Trends That Will Change the Future of Publishing
126

Philip Ruppel

E-books are rapidly growing in popularity, and the future e-book market will involve e-books that offer many interactive features and can be read on a few winners in the e-reader war. Publishers will have an important role in providing the content of interactive e-books.

E-books Will Change the Textbook Business
130

Jeffrey R. Young

An e-textbook revolution is on the horizon. Textbook publishers and college leaders are proposing a new model that involves colleges buying e-textbooks in bulk and then charging students a course materials fee.

E-books May Result in the End of Libraries as Book-Lending Institutions
136

Jonathan Rochkind

Libraries must get publishers' permission to lend out e-books, and publishers can charge what they want for this—a scenario that threatens the existence of libraries as book lenders.

Organizations to Contact
140

Bibliography
144

Index
149

Foreword

By definition, controversies are "discussions of questions in which opposing opinions clash" (*Webster's Twentieth Century Dictionary Unabridged*). Few would deny that controversies are a pervasive part of the human condition and exist on virtually every level of human enterprise. Controversies transpire between individuals and among groups, within nations and between nations. Controversies supply the grist necessary for progress by providing challenges and challengers to the status quo. They also create atmospheres where strife and warfare can flourish. A world without controversies would be a peaceful world; but it also would be, by and large, static and prosaic.

The Series' Purpose

The purpose of the Current Controversies series is to explore many of the social, political, and economic controversies dominating the national and international scenes today. Titles selected for inclusion in the series are highly focused and specific. For example, from the larger category of criminal justice, Current Controversies deals with specific topics such as police brutality, gun control, white collar crime, and others. The debates in Current Controversies also are presented in a useful, timeless fashion. Articles and book excerpts included in each title are selected if they contribute valuable, long-range ideas to the overall debate. And wherever possible, current information is enhanced with historical documents and other relevant materials. Thus, while individual titles are current in focus, every effort is made to ensure that they will not become quickly outdated. Books in the Current Controversies series will remain important resources for librarians, teachers, and students for many years.

In addition to keeping the titles focused and specific, great care is taken in the editorial format of each book in the series. Book introductions and chapter prefaces are offered to provide background material for readers. Chapters are organized around several key questions that are answered with diverse opinions representing all points on the political spectrum. Materials in each chapter include opinions in which authors clearly disagree as well as alternative opinions in which authors may agree on a broader issue but disagree on the possible solutions. In this way, the content of each volume in Current Controversies mirrors the mosaic of opinions encountered in society. Readers will quickly realize that there are many viable answers to these complex issues. By questioning each author's conclusions, students and casual readers can begin to develop the critical thinking skills so important to evaluating opinionated material.

Current Controversies is also ideal for controlled research. Each anthology in the series is composed of primary sources taken from a wide gamut of informational categories including periodicals, newspapers, books, US and foreign government documents, and the publications of private and public organizations. Readers will find factual support for reports, debates, and research papers covering all areas of important issues. In addition, an annotated table of contents, an index, a book and periodical bibliography, and a list of organizations to contact are included in each book to expedite further research.

Perhaps more than ever before in history, people are confronted with diverse and contradictory information. During the Persian Gulf War, for example, the public was not only treated to minute-to-minute coverage of the war, it was also inundated with critiques of the coverage and countless analyses of the factors motivating US involvement. Being able to sort through the plethora of opinions accompanying today's major issues, and to draw one's own conclusions, can be a complicated and frustrating struggle. It is the editors' hope that Current Controversies will help readers with this struggle.

Introduction

Introduced for mass markets during the early 2000s, e-books remain controversial within the publishing world, but they have been a big hit with the public.

Electronic books, often called e-books, are books in a digital format that can only be read on e-readers—devices such as Amazon's Kindle or Apple's iPad—or on computers or mobile phones. Sometimes, e-books are simply digital versions of printed books, but increasingly, e-books are being written and sold online without ever being published as a traditional paper book. Introduced for mass markets during the early 2000s, e-books remain controversial within the publishing world, but they have been a big hit with the public. Demand for e-books has exploded year after year, and in 2010 the online bookseller Amazon reported that it had sold more e-books than printed books for the first time ever. The history of e-books is a short one so far, but many technology observers believe that the future of this new medium is bright.

The first e-books were created decades ago, but commercial e-book sales did not take off until the first decade of the twenty-first century. The first person to develop an electronic book was an Italian Jesuit priest, Father Roberto Busa (1913–2011), who in the 1940s began a project to build an electronic index to the works of Saint Thomas Aquinas. The purpose was to allow religious scholars to do research using text searches. A CD-ROM version was finally completed in 1989, and a Web version followed. The first person to use the term electronic book, however, was the computer science professor, Andries van Dam, who was born in the Netherlands in 1938 and who headed a project at Brown University in the 1960s to create a hypertext system that allowed documents and books to be typeset in digital format. Van Dam's system, called FRESS, was used by the Brown faculty, and van Dam later developed other electronic book systems for the Navy and other parties.

Many technology observers, however, credit American author Michael S. Hart (1947–2011) with the invention of the e-book as it came to be known. In 1971, Hart acquired access to the mainframe computer at the University of Illinois, and he used this opportunity to create the first free e-book: a downloadable version of the US Declaration of Independence. This was the beginning of Project Gutenberg, an effort by Hart to create electronic copies of various books and distribute them to the public for free. The project is named after Johannes Gutenberg (c.1398–1468), a German printer who invented the movable type printing press. Over the years, Project Gutenberg created digitized versions of the Bible, technical and reference manuals, cookbooks, as well as thousands of novels, short stories, and periodicals. Following Hart's death, Project Gutenberg continued and, as of 2011, had digitized over 38,000 titles.

Before the Internet, early e-books were written mostly for small scholarly or special interest markets and were stored on CDs that could be read on computers. The growing availability of the Internet, beginning in the 1990s, however, made it easy to download e-books, launching a competition among companies to produce e-readers. The result was a profusion of types of e-readers that used various formats. The standards association, the International Digital Publishing Forum (IDPF), was eventually set up to establish a single usable format for e-book publishing, and in 1999 the group developed the Open eBook Publication Structure (OEBPS) as the official e-book standard. In 2007, this earlier format was superseded by Electronic Publication (EPUB), the early 2000s standard format for e-books. However, some online e-book sources also use a PDF format, which is a common format for downloading documents from the Internet. As of 2012, the top-selling e-readers are the Amazon Kindle, which does not use EPUB or PDF but can be converted into EPUB, and Apple's iPad, which allows the use of either EPUB or PDF formats.

During the early 2000s, e-books became ubiquitous. Many books in the public domain (copyright free by having been published before 1923) or whose copyrights have otherwise expired have been published as e-books. Google Books, a project of the Internet search company Google, has made many public domain books available on its website, for example. At the same time, the online bookseller Amazon began selling e-book versions of printed books at deep discounts, and it also allowed writers to self-publish their writings as e-books directly on its website, circumventing the traditional publishing companies that historically have acted as gatekeepers in the publishing world. In addition, many libraries across the country began purchasing and lending e-books to the public.

Year after year, the popularity of e-books has increased, with readers buying more and more e-books and pushing libraries to offer more e-book titles. This e-book demand, however, has created controversy within the publishing world, with book publishers worrying about whether e-books might someday overtake printed books and jockeying to protect both their position as e-book publishers and their profit margins. The authors of viewpoints offered in this book, *Current Controversies: E-books*, discuss some of the issues in the e-book debate, including whether e-books are better than printed books, whether libraries should buy and lend e-books, how e-books should be priced for libraries and the public, and what the future might hold for the e-book market.

CHAPTER 1

Are E-books Better than Paper Books?

Chapter Preface

Perhaps the biggest drawback to e-books is that, unlike printed books, they require the use of an electronic device, typically an e-reader or a tablet. Many consumers find these devices expensive, and choosing among many products can be tricky. Three companies lead the market (Amazon, Apple, and Barnes & Noble), but a few other companies also sell e-readers and tablets.

Consumers must first decide whether to purchase an e-reader or a tablet. An e-ink reader is the cheapest choice, and often the best one for consumers who only want to be able to read e-books and possibly some newspapers and magazines. Priced at $49 to $149, e-ink readers show only black and white print, are generally about the size of a hardcover book, and provide the closest experience to reading a printed book. The fonts can be enlarged and changed to make reading easier, even though the screen is quite small. Also, unlike tablets, basic e-readers are lightweight, an important consideration for people who spend hours reading. An added advantage is that these devices use e-ink screen technology, which allows them to be read in bright sunlight. However, these low-end readers cannot be used to surf the Internet, play games, or send emails. As of 2012, the leading basic e-readers are the Amazon Kindle (about $79), the Amazon Kindle Touch (about $99 to $189 with a touchscreen), and the Barnes & Noble Nook Simple Touch (about $99 with a touchscreen).

For consumers who want additional computer features, the better choice may be a tablet. In addition to functioning more like a laptop computer and as a reader for e-books, tablets also typically are larger than e-readers and offer a color screen. Another advantage is that they are backlit so, unlike e-readers, tablets can be read in the dark. The main drawbacks to tablets, however, are their cost ($400 and up) and the fact that they use an LCD screen, which cannot be read in sunlight. In addition, many popular tablets are bigger and heavier than most e-readers, and reading an LCD screen for a long time can cause eye strain. The top-selling tablets are the Apple iPad and the Apple iPad 2. Some companies have tried to combine the best of these two devices by offering smaller, less expensive versions of tablet readers—typically sized like e-readers but with LCD screens, the ability to perform some computer functions, and priced from about $199 to $249, about half the price of full-sized tablets. Examples of these smaller tablets are the Amazon Kindle Fire and the Barnes & Noble Nook Tablet. All tablets come with touchscreens, like many basic e-readers.

Consumers also need to decide whether to buy versions that use Wi-Fi, which requires users to be near an accessible Wi-Fi area to download books or access the Internet, or that use the newer 3G/4G service, which is a cellular wireless network that can be accessed most of the time from almost anywhere. Wi-Fi, of course, is much cheaper, and, for most readers, probably adequate because once books are downloaded, they are stored on the e-reader and can be read at any time. However, for people who like having instant access to newspapers, email, or social networking sites, or who travel much of the time, paying a monthly premium fee for a 3G or 4G network may be acceptable. The Kindle Fire and Nook Simple Touch are only available in Wi-Fi versions, and the Kindle Touch is offered with a 3G wireless package that is limited to downloading books, magazines, and newspapers. Tablets more typically use 3G or 4G access; the iPad, for example, is available both in Wi-Fi and in 3G and 4G from Verizon and AT&T wireless providers. Fortunately, these providers do not require long-term contracts, and consumers can cancel or restart service at any time.

A final consideration for consumers is how easily e-books can be downloaded and moved between different devices.

Cloud technology allows stored e-books to be easily read on a variety of devices, including mobile phones and computers, and free applications are available that allow readers to purchase and read e-books from the many different e-book sellers. Also, some e-book sellers offer more flexibility than others. For example, Kindle books from Amazon and Nook books from Barnes & Noble can be read on most Apple, Android, and Blackberry devices, and on PC and Mac computers. Apple's iBooks, however, can only be read on Apple devices. In addition, all e-readers and tablets can be used to check out e-books from libraries, although special free software may be needed to do so.

For some traditional readers, however, the best way to read books is by holding the paper version in their hands. The authors of viewpoints included in this chapter discuss whether e-books are better than paper books.

E-books Have Many Advantages Compared to Traditional Books

Jason Cross and Melissa J. Perenson

Jason Cross and Melissa J. Perenson are writers for PCWorld, *the established leader for news, reviews, and insight on the PC ecosystem.*

As consumer interest in e-book readers approaches critical mass, the number of high-quality models available is mushrooming.

What Are the Benefits and Advantages of E-books?

The e-book universe is expanding vapidly. Amazon's Kindles still offer the ultimate in wircless-transfer convenience, but other readers and e-book resellers are starting to compete on price and content—including hundreds of thousands of free books Amazon doesn't offer.

E-books have numerous benefits. Eliminating paper saves resources. E-book readers take up little room in travelers' backpacks and purses, while storing the equivalent of a whole bookshelf. You don't have to go anywhere to buy or borrow an e-book title. For the vision-impaired, the ability to adjust font size can make the difference between being able to read a book and having to hope for an audio version. Some readers double as music players, and some even read books aloud.

What Is the Future of E-books?

Unfortunately, the world of e-books is Balkanized, with multiple incompatible file formats and digital rights management

Jason Cross and Melissa J. Perenson, "The E-Book Explosion," *PC World*, Volume 27, Issue 12, December 2009, pp. 44–48. Copyright © 2009 by PC World. All rights reserved. Reproduced by permission.

(DRM) technologies, and devices with varying support for both. Books in the public domain are widely available in PDF and other standard formats. But copyrighted material is another story. Amazon's current Kindles can obtain commercial e-books in Amazon's AZW file format via wireless download only in the United States (in early October [2009], however, the company announced a Kindle capable of downloading content in most countries).

Meanwhile, Sony, which produces some of the classiest e-book readers around, is abandoning its proprietary BBeB e-book file format and shifting protected content in its e-book store to Adobe ePub, an e-book file format that book publishers and resellers have widely embraced. Whereas Adobe's PDF reproduces a fixed image of a page, ePub permits reflowing of text to accommodate different fonts and font sizes.

Adobe offers a DRM technology called Adobe Content Server 4. Sony and a number of other online bookstores—most notably Borders—sell commercial titles in ePub/ ACS4 format, and some libraries let patrons check out ePub books. As of early October, 17 e-book readers supported ePub and ACS4, making that combination the closest thing the industry has to a standard for DRM-protected books. Aside from the Amazon Kindles and Foxit's eSlick, all of the e-book readers in this review support ePub/ACS4.

A Few Available E-readers

1. Sony Reader Touch Edition. Sony's new flagship e-book reader offers something we haven't seen in previous Sony Readers: a touchscreen and stylus for navigating and for creating drawings and handwritten notes. Whether this innovation enhances the e-book experience is open to debate, but the overall quality of the product is not: Except for its lack of wireless connectivity for purchasing books without connecting to a PC, the Touch Edition is a worthy competitor to Amazon's

Kindles. The Touch Edition lets you create text memos (via an on-screen keyboard), listen to unprotected MP3 and AAC music, view images, and set up a slideshow. The MP3 player was the best on any e-book reader I tried, with reasonably strong audio through earphones plugged into the Touch Edition's standard headphone jack. It includes repeat/shuffle options, and you can play the music while you read. The reader comes with a dictionary and lets you annotate your books and documents.

2. Amazon Kindle DX. The Kindle DX looks surprisingly lean and elegant. At 7.2 by 10.4 by 0.4 inches and 18.9 ounces, the Kindle DX is the largest and heaviest of today's e-book readers. Like the Kindle 2, it has a keyboard (for annotations and for searching for books in Amazon's Kindle store through the built-in wireless connection), but typing on it is awkward. In the United States you can shop for and download books from the device without connecting to a PC (only the just-announced global version of the Kindle 2 lets you download content elsewhere). Though the DX's spacious screen and skinny profile are big pluses, the device is unlikely to succeed as a newspaper or magazine replacement; it's too heavy for that, and its E Ink display lacks the color and visual appeal that modern print publications possess.

3. Amazon Kindle 2. The Kindle 2 is a sleek, curved tablet that you can hold easily in your hands. Like other Kindles, it offers easy access to Amazon's Kindle store through Sprint's 3G wireless network (at no extra cost to users), so shopping for books is a breeze. But Amazon doesn't make available the hundreds of thousands of free e-books you can get from other stores. Its polished design looks great, as does its 6-inch, 600-by-800-pixel E

Ink screen. Text is sharp, and images are crisp. Even though its extras are limited to a text-to-speech capability, a basic MP3 player, and a Web browser, the Kindle 2 stands as a good reader's companion overall.

4. Sony Reader Pocket Edition. The Pocket Edition is about as inexpensive as e-book readers come. It lacks extras that some competitors offer, but its topflight design and usability more than compensate for the missing features. Like previous Sony Readers, the Pocket Edition has a metal case (most competitors use some sort of plastic), which may explain why it tips the scales at nearly half a pound. But the silvery case felt great in my hands, and the reader's controls are simple and intuitive. Reading on the Pocket Edition is easy and intuitive: Pages looked good and flowed neatly, and page turns were responsive—on a par with those of other devices. Overall, the Pocket Edition is appealing, not just for people on a budget (after all, the Kindle isn't a lot more expensive), but for anyone who wants a small, no-frills e-book reader to carry in a purse or backpack.

5. Interead Cool-ER. The Cool-ER strives to distinguish itself from the black-and-gray competition, and for the most part it succeeds. Skinny (0.4 inch thick), lightweight (6.2 ounces) and available in eight cheery colors, this e-book resembles an overgrown iPod—not a bad role model for industrial design. The only items visible below the 6-inch screen are the device's logo and a round, iPod-esque four-way navigation/selection wheel, which you use to navigate through menus and turn pages. Unfortunately, because the button is quite stiff, using it is unnecessarily arduous. The Cool-ER's display employs the same E Ink technology that Kindles, Sony Readers, and other e-book readers use. You can transfer content only via the USB cable, but a wireless model is

due next year. The built-in MP3 player lets you play music while you read, but it's a barebones audio player. Annoyingly, the headphone jack port doesn't accept standard mobile 3.5mm jacks. You'll have to get a 2.5mm adapter to use it with most current headphones or phone headsets (the Cool-ER comes without earphones). A little polish (and a better four-way navigation wheel) would improve the Cool-ER's usability. But for the price, it's not a bad deal.

E-books Have Great Benefits for Academic and Research Libraries

Sue Polanka

Sue Polanka is head of reference and instruction at Wright State University Libraries and the editor of No Shelf Required: E-Books in Libraries.

According to a survey conducted by the Chief Officers of State Library Agencies (COSLA) in the summer of 2011, 39 percent of public libraries had not begun to offer downloadable media service (ebooks, audiobooks, movies) to their communities. COSLA reported that small, rural libraries with limited budgets were most likely not to have access to downloadable media.

COSLA believes that ebooks will be the preferred format for reading materials in the future. As a result, it has set a goal for all U.S. public libraries to offer ebooks and downloadable media by 2015.

Why Buy Ebooks?

There are a variety of reasons for purchasing ebooks, and the first is access. Offering ebooks extends content beyond the physical boundaries of the library. In a digital world, patrons aren't restricted to brick-and-mortar hours. They can choose to download a new book late Sunday evening because content is available 24/7.

Furthermore, there has been an explosion of interest in ebooks and ereaders. The Pew Internet & American Life Project released research findings in January [2012] stating

Sue Polanka, "An Ebook Primer," *Library Journal*, Volume 137, Issue 7, April 15, 2012, pp. 42–44. Copyright © 2012 by Library Journals LLC. All rights reserved. Reproduced by permission.

that "[t]he number of Americans owning at least one of these digital reading devices (tablets or ereaders) jumped from 18 percent in December to 29 percent in January." This has put demands on public libraries for not only digital content but also technical support for downloading content to devices. Additionally, there is no physical space required for ebooks. Virtual bookshelves don't require weeding and shifting. The fear of loss of or damage to content also diminishes.

That said, ebooks have just as many reasons not to be purchased. They are more expensive than print, and their use is restricted with digital rights management (DRM). Content is often leased rather than owned owing to vendor license agreements. Moreover, annual fees are often required to guarantee perpetual access to content. The business models are much different from print models. Often, they are unsustainable for public library budgets. Publisher content may not be available for library lending—Macmillan, Simon & Schuster, Hachette, and Penguin Group (the last of which ended its OverDrive contract on February 9 [2012]) do not sell ebooks to libraries or library vendors. In addition, Random House raised its prices on March 1, in some cases tripling the cost of an ebook for libraries. Ebooks also require technology in order for the user to read them. If readers in one's community have no access to that technology—ereaders, tablet devices, smartphones, or personal computers—they will be shut out of the ebook environment.

Community Involvement

Before you decide to purchase ebooks for your library, consider surveying your community about their needs. Are your patrons asking for ebooks? If so, what type of content do they desire—best-selling fiction, children's books, reference materials, or perhaps classic literature? What type of reading devices are they using—Amazon Kindles, Barnes & Noble Nooks, or Apple iPads, smartphones, or personal computers? This information will guide decisions about content and format, as well as keep the community involved in shaping a digital collection.

Many libraries have created spreadsheets or matrixes to compare features quickly.

Free and Fee-based Ebook Content

For libraries with limited budgets, locating free ebook content is essential. The good news is that you have options. The bad news is that they are not the titles on the *New York Times's* best sellers list. Nonetheless, there are thousands of sources for free ebooks available online. Just be certain you aren't downloading pirated content, which is often found on large peer-to-peer file-sharing sites.

When the time does come to purchase ebook content, public libraries have a variety of choices. It's important to evaluate all of the vendors, determine the expense and licensing of each, and calculate ongoing costs to determine if the model selected is sustainable.

If your library is looking to purchase reference ebooks or scholarly content, there are several possibilities. You may purchase using an aggregator (a vendor that sells titles from multiple publishers on a single platform), by going direct to the publisher on the publisher's platform, or through a distributor (a vendor that sells print and ebooks from multiple publishers and/or aggregators). Titles and prices vary by vendor, size of library, and number of simultaneous users. Content from these vendors is designed primarily for online reading. The interfaces are intended to be quite robust, with a suite of features. It is possible to download reference articles, book chapters, or entire titles for offline reading from the majority of these vendors. Policies and procedures will vary.

Evaluating Vendors

When purchasing ebooks and other downloadable media, it is crucial to evaluate each vendor. Many libraries have created spreadsheets or matrixes to compare features quickly. Some things that should be compared include content/titles available, format of files, business models and costs, licensing terms (ownership or access), ongoing fees, MARC [Machine-Readable Cataloging] record availability and cost, download options, printing, interface features, customer support and training, and use data. Several libraries have posted sample evaluation charts online.

Downloading Content

Most patrons will want to download library ebooks to a personal reading device. Therefore, it's imperative that libraries understand file formats, devices, and download procedures. This can be very complicated given the many file formats and ereading devices on the market. Generally, ebooks will be sold to libraries in PDF or EPUB file format. These formats are supported by many reading devices like the Nook, Sony Reader, Kobo, iPad, and many reading applications for tablet devices and smartphones. Kindles, on the other hand, use a proprietary format known as AZW. As mentioned earlier, OverDrive is the only library vendor to offer direct downloads to Kindles. The Kindle process is relatively simple and smooth, using a patron's Amazon account as the delivery source for content once it is checked out from the library.

For most ebook downloads, however, the process involves additional steps. First, patrons must find the title they want by searching the library OPAC [online public access catalog], or the digital library site provided by the vendor. Once a title is selected, it must be checked out using one's library card. Titles purchased with unlimited simultaneous use, or those in the public domain, may not require this, as multiple users can access them at the same time.

After the title is checked out, patrons download the file onto a computer or tablet device using software or an application (app). The predominant software for this download is Adobe Digital Editions (ADE). ADE is free but requires a user to register and download the software onto a personal computer. ADE can be used to store, organize, and read content. It can also be used to transfer downloaded titles to an ereading device through the USB port. To complete the transfer, ereading devices must be registered to an ADE account.

The first time a patron downloads a library ebook is always the most complicated, as software must be downloaded and registered. Once these steps are completed, repeating the process becomes, well, less complicated. Many library users (and librarians) may be overwhelmed by the download process and give up. Technical difficulties can occur at any time, and often do.

A Helping Hand

If you plan to provide downloadable ebooks as a service, you need to offer training and support for your staff. In turn, the staff will need to provide training and support to their patrons.

Libraries across the country are supporting hands-on training sessions, video tutorials, demonstrations, or documentation to patrons. Much of this material is available online, either from public library websites, YouTube, or vendor sites. Many library vendors have extensive training and support programs for their member libraries as well.

The best training, however, is experimentation. Encourage staff to practice downloading ebooks to library or personal computers. If your library can afford it, purchase several different ereading devices for the staff. These can be used for hands-on training with both staff or patrons.

Another interesting idea that has been successful at both Douglas County Libraries, CO, and Dayton Metro Libraries

[Ohio] is a rebate plan to staff who purchase personal ereading devices. Both organizations worked with their library boards or Friends groups to provide $50 rebates for those purchases. Jamie LaRue, director of Douglas County Libraries, told me last year that, as a result of the rebate program, his staff started having impromptu discussion groups at lunch. They shared tips and techniques with one another and experimented with the various devices.

The Bottom Line

Determining how much of one's materials budget to spend on ebooks will vary with each library. As mentioned earlier, be aware of your community's needs for electronic content and make budget decisions based on those needs. You can always start small with a pilot program and expand if demand grows.

Demand for ebooks in public libraries is present, growing, and not likely to stop anytime soon, and 2015 is just around the corner. If you aren't on the bus, it's time to buy your ticket. Just grab a rail and hang on, because it's going to be a wild ride.

E-books Allow Authors to Self-Publish Easily

Bethany Ramos

Bethany Ramos is a freelance writer and book author.

The publishing industry is definitely changing, and today, these great changes center around e-books. Even the hottest bestsellers on the shelves are being formatted to e-readers so that they can be enjoyed by readers anywhere on devices like the Kindle.

Speedy Publishing Process

Perhaps one of the greatest benefits to e-reader publishing is that it is electronic and virtually instantaneous. Books that are formatted to e-readers can be sold and downloaded from websites like Amazon, so they potentially reach an even greater reader base. For the many readers out there that are interested in a new book but don't want to go to the bookstore or library to get it, all they have to do is download the publication to their e-reader in a few moments. This puts quick money in the pocket of the author to generate even greater online sales.

How Does E-reader Publishing Work?

If you're interested in publishing your book to an e-reader through a website like Amazon, you will firstly need an Amazon account. There you will find a prompt to publish on the Kindle by using the digital text platform available through Amazon.

If you are self-publishing to an e-reader, it is important that your book is completely edited before publishing. Amazon does not edit any publications for the Kindle, so ensuring that your book is up to par is your responsibility. This editing should be much more than just running a spellcheck. Make sure that you and several trusted people in your life have read through the book numerous times to ensure that it is in its best condition.

From there, Amazon will allow you to upload your e-book as a word document, text file, PDF, or HTML. However, it is best to only use PDF as a last resort since it may be difficult to format for the Kindle. You can then upload your book to the Amazon digital text platform, where you will be redirected to a dashboard to help you publish your book directly. One handy feature is that you don't have to publish your book immediately; you can upload it and leave it on the dashboard as a draft until you are ready for the final publication.

Once your book is ready for publication, you can publish it to e-reader format with the simple click of a button. Your e-reader book will be available for purchase on Amazon within 72 hours, and you can view your sales and downloads directly through the Amazon dashboard.

This is a similar process that publishing houses now use to convert best-selling books into the e-reader format. Perhaps one of the greatest benefits to publishing to the Kindle is that any author has the opportunity to share their work with the world. If you are interested in self-publishing, then an e-reader publication may be the best choice for you.

Making your work available online in the digital format will help you to reach new reader bases that you may not have been able to market to if your book was in the traditional form!

Paper Books Are Still the Best Way to Read Books

Eric Sammons

Eric Sammons is the director of evangelization for the Diocese of Venice in Florida, a blogger, and author of several books on Catholicism.

The "must-have" gadget this Christmas season [2009] is clearly the e-reader. The Amazon Kindle appears to be flying off the shelves, and the Barnes and Noble Nook is backordered due to high demand. As a self-professed bibliophile, I have followed the development of e-books with great interest, and even with some concern. At first, my Luddite tendencies prevailed and I thought e-readers were a silly fad, but then for a while my geek side won out and I embraced the concept wholeheartedly. But then I began to question some of the outlandish statements made on their behalf, especially the belief that they will completely replace paper-bound books in the near future. This is not going to happen.

The reason I don't think e-readers will replace paper-bound books isn't simply nostalgia; it is an opinion based on technology. And simply put, *the paper-bound book is a vastly superior technology compared to the current e-readers.* The e-reader is better at some specific tasks, but in most ways, the paper-bound book still offers the best way to read books.

Here are a few ways in which the paper-bound book is superior to the e-reader:

1. *A common, lasting format.* Currently, the e-reader market is in the classic "Beta vs. VHS" stage. Getting a book on a Kindle doesn't mean that you could read it on a

Nook. There is no clear-cut winner yet in the format wars, so the reader you get now may not be able to read any e-books in five or ten years. Even if the manufacturers of e-readers would agree on a common format, you still must possess an e-reader of some kind to read an e-book. Anyone can read a paper-bound book, however.

2. *Easier to share.* The Nook has a unique feature that allows you to "lend" your e-books to another e-reader for 14 days (and then, for some inexplicable reason, you can't re-loan it to them). This is considered advanced in the e-reader field, but it is clearly far inferior to the paper-bound book world, where you can lend your books to anyone you want (they don't need a compatible e-reader or any device, for that matter) and for as long as you want.

3. *More resistance to damage.* Ever thought about reading a book in the bath? Good luck if you have an e-reader. Also, if you run over a Kindle with your car, you have to purchase a whole new Kindle and re-download all your books. Running over a book with your car usually just puts a tire-mark on it, especially if it is a hard-back.

4. *Longer-lasting.* A paper-bound book can outlast the lifespan of a human being. The typical lifespan of a high-tech device is about 2–5 years. Once you are on the e-book track, you will need to constantly keep upgrading over the course of your life to maintain that lifestyle.

5. *True ownership.* If you buy a book, you own it. Forever. When you buy an e-book, you are just licensing the text from Amazon or the publisher or whoever truly owns the book. If they want, they can take away your e-book for any reason or no reason (which has already happened once with the Kindle).

6. *Superior reading experience.* This is not as subjective as it sounds. When you read a paper-bound book, you are using more than your sense of sight. You are also using your sense of touch. You know just by holding the book how far along you are—there is no need to check the page indicator at the bottom of a screen. Furthermore, if you need to go back a few pages to remember who a character is or review an important point made by the author, flipping back a few pages while skimming the text is quite easy—at least in comparison to doing the same on an e-reader. Studies have shown that paper allows people to process text better than text on a screen.

7. *More focused reading.* When you are reading a paper-bound book, there is nothing else you can do with that book. Your entire attention is focused on the text and on nothing else. With an e-reader, you can quickly change to another book or even on some readers decide to browse the web. (Some have noticed that this lack of focus with screen reading is changing how we think). The single-mindedness of the paper-bound book has been called a disadvantage by some, but it is clearly an advantage if you really want to engage the text of the book. Both this point and #6 above leads to a "deeper" reading experience: you can engage the text more closely and in a more focused manner than you can in an e-reader.

This is not to say that the e-reader is worthless; on the contrary, it has many positive features that make it useful for certain types of reading. For example, I often will print out long PDF's I find online so that I can read them away from my computer. This has led to piles of paper crammed throughout my office. I can see the benefit of just loading these on an e-reader. The same thing could be said for magazines—do we really need a bunch of paper magazines sitting around the house? Also, I can see much benefit to an e-reader for college students. Instead of lugging around 50 lbs of books that cost north of $500—books that will probably never been read again by that student—just putting it all on an e-reader can be quite helpful.

But these are specific cases and don't encompass the whole reading experience. At least for a while, the most "high-tech" way to read a book is the old-fashioned way: paper-bound books.

E-books Will Widen the Digital Divide

Christopher Mims

Christopher Mims is a journalist who writes about technology, sustainability, energy, and climate change.

Today [September 21, 2011] Amazon announced that it is finally rolling out Kindle-compatible ebooks to public libraries in the U.S., a much-needed evolution of the dominant e-reading platform. But there's a larger problem that this development fails to address, and it's an issue exacerbated by every part of Amazon's business model.

Access to Knowledge

Access to knowledge has long been seen as vital to the public interest—literally, in economic parlance, a "public good"—which is why libraries have always been supported through taxes and philanthropy.

I challenge anyone reading this to recall his or her earliest experiences with books—nearly all of which, I'm willing to bet, were second-hand, passed on by family members or purchased in that condition. Now consider that the eBook completely eliminates both the secondary book market and any control that libraries—i.e. the public—has over the copies of a text it has purchased.

Except under limited circumstances, eBooks cannot be loaned or resold. They cannot be gifted, nor discovered on a trip through the shelves of a friend or the local library. They cannot be re-bound and, unlike all the rediscovered works that literally gave birth to the Renaissance, they will not last for centuries. Indeed, publishers are already limiting the number of times a library can loan out an eBook to 26.

If the transition to eBooks is complete—and with libraries being among the most significant buyers of books, it now seems inevitable—the flexibility of book ownership will be gone forever. Knowledge, in as much as books represent it, will belong to someone else.

Unlike books, . . . e-books put additional barriers between readers and knowledge.

The Need for E-readers

Worse yet, there is the problem of the e-reader itself. This issue may be resolved by falling prices of e-readers, but there remains the possibility that the demands of profitability will drive makers of e-readers to simply set a floor on the price they're willing to charge for one and attempt to continually innovate toward tablet-like functionality in order to justify that price.

Unlike books, which are one of the few media that do not require a secondary external device for playback, e-books put additional barriers between readers and knowledge. Some of those barriers, as I've mentioned, consist of Digital Rights Management [technology that prevents an e-book from being copied] and other attempts to use intellectual property laws as a kind of rent-seeking, but others are more subtle.

One in five children in the U.S. lives below the poverty line, and those numbers are likely to increase as the world economy continues to work through a painful de-leveraging of accrued debt. In the past, the only thing a child needed to read a book was basic literacy, something that our public education system in theory still provides.

Imagine Abraham Lincoln, born in a log cabin, raised in poverty, self-taught from a small cache of books, being stymied in his early education by the lack of an e-reader. And there are countless other examples—in his biography, [singer-songwriter] Bob Dylan recounts spending his first, penniless days in New York City lost in a friend's library of classics, reading and re-reading the greatest poets of history as he found his own voice.

Sure, these are extreme examples, but it is undeniable that books have a democratizing effect on learning. They are inherently amenable to the frictionless dissemination of information. Durable and cheap to produce, to the point of disposability, their abundance, which we currently take for granted, has been a constant and invisible force for the creation of an informed citizenry.

So the question becomes: Do we want books to become subject to the 'digital divide?' Is that really wise, given the trajectory of the 21st century?

E-books Are Not Greener than Paper Books

Sierra Club Green Home

Sierra Club Green Home is a website created by the environmental group Sierra Club, designed to help Americans create healthier environments in their homes and make them more energy efficient.

A relatively new phenomenon is the E-Reader, be it Kindle, iPad, or a number of other new competitors coming into the marketplace. When you think about it, these devices would seem to be more environmentally friendly than your typical paper and cardboard book, even a paperback. Should we be buying our loved ones e-readers or traditional books this holiday season?

There is a certain tactile value to "real" books, just feeling the paper, turning the pages. I find that I miss this when using an e-reader. But on the surface, the e-reader would seem to be much more green. In fact, my colleague "Mr. Green" at *Sierra Magazine* recently explored this dilemma and came to a surprising conclusion, which I will reveal momentarily.

The Green Rating for E-books

E-reader vs. paper book is a provocative question, one that could just as easily have been "do your prefer flying cars or conventional road going cars" a few short years ago. The key to the answer is that basic tenet of sustainability, life cycle analysis. We must consider not only the trees needed to make paper versus the manufacturing of electronics products, but the shipping costs, fuel, and ultimately, the energy needed to recycle these materials at the end of their days. Not to mention, what ultimately happens to e-waste. Where do the non-recyclable remains end up?

Mr. Green's conclusion—as well as a recent *New York Times* piece on the same subject—was that unless you're a fast and furious reader, the energy required to manufacture and then dispose of an e-reader is probably greater than what's needed to make a traditional book. If you're reading 40 or more books per year on your e-reader, that would be the right choice. But if you use it only occasionally, probably better to stick to a "regular" book. This conclusion is reinforced by a study referenced on the website of TerraPass, a carbon offset business. Unfortunately, the study itself is not available for publication but its authors said e-readers are the more environmentally responsible choice only if you are reading in excess of 23 books per year.

The *New York Times* article also explored this subject, with a slightly different conclusion. Using similar data, an outfit called Cleantech did a study which looked at the question sort of in reverse, saying if you were to read three books a month over four years, the e-reader would significantly outperform conventional paper books in carbon emitted.

Clearly, like many green subjects, ours is a young industry, and as such, definitive answers are hard to come by. At least, subject to interpretation. Either way, I hope that today's generation will read more and watch less, be it through paper or electronic means.

Here's the best answer, though: go to the public library next time you are downtown. Borrow three or four books, finish them all, then return 'em next time you're near the library. This is truly the most sustainable way to read: the good old fashioned public library. At Sierra Club Green Home, we preach "reduce, reuse, and recycle" and library books can be read by dozens of people over their lifetime. And once they are finally too dog-eared and beaten up to grace library shelves, they can be easily recycled since they are generally all paper (even the leather on deluxe bound editions can be recycled).

CHAPTER 2

Should Libraries Buy and Lend E-books?

Chapter Preface

E-books have been growing in popularity in recent years, and libraries want to offer e-books to library users; however, e-book publishers are reluctant to sell e-books to libraries under the same conditions as printed books. Libraries typically lend printed books to one person at a time for a limited period, but because e-books are digital, it is possible for them to be lent by libraries to unlimited numbers of readers simultaneously. Publishers are, therefore, concerned that if libraries can buy e-books and freely lend them out, consumers will simply check out e-books from libraries and will have no incentive to buy e-books from e-book publishers. Such a scenario could seriously harm publishers' profits in the e-book market. As of 2012, the resulting conflict between libraries and book publishers has continued, with no clear resolution in sight.

Under the first-sale doctrine, libraries traditionally have been legally allowed to lend out printed books as many times as they want once they purchase the book from the publisher. Often, libraries purchase multiple copies of bestsellers, and once the demand for those titles falls, libraries place those books in used-book sales in order to regain part of their initial cost. E-books, however, are not covered by the first-sale policy, so publishers have yet to find an e-book policy for libraries that is acceptable to both sides. As of 2012, the six largest book publishers in the United States (HarperCollins, Random House, Macmillan, Simon & Schuster, Penguin Group, and Hachette Book Group) either charge high prices or limit or completely refuse to sell e-books to libraries.

The two major book publishers that do continue to sell e-books to libraries (HarperCollins and Random House) have taken dramatically different approaches. HarperCollins shocked the library world in March 2011 by implementing new e-book restrictions for libraries, basically requiring that e-books can be checked out only 26 times before the license expires. Random House continues to sell e-books to libraries but has raised its prices, tripling the cost of e-books for this market. E-books that once cost libraries $40 shot up to $120, for example, just at a time when many public libraries are facing budget constraints due to economic recession and government funding cuts. Other major publishers, as well as many smaller publishers, simply refuse to sell e-books to libraries or else make only a few e-book titles available for library lending.

A number of libraries and library consortiums initially responded to publisher e-book restrictions by boycotting those publishers, but the boycott shows signs of weakening. The American Library Association has been working with publishers to find a solution, and some libraries are finding that the HarperCollins model may be more workable than first thought. Commentators have called for Congress to resolve the matter by passing legislation giving libraries greater rights to digital books, but Congress may be unwilling or unable to do so. How this situation will develop is difficult to predict, but it is clear that consumers will continue to demand e-books and will get them wherever they can.

Meanwhile, many observers say that libraries are facing threats from other players in the e-book market. Late in 2011, for example, the online bookseller Amazon announced it was launching its own e-book lending library for members of its Amazon Prime Service. Subscribers to this service pay $79 per year and are allowed to borrow one e-book at a time from Amazon with no due dates. Some people have speculated that other companies, such as iPad manufacturer Apple or e-reader manufacturer Barnes & Noble, might follow Amazon's lead in creating lending policies. Some librarians, therefore, fear that the e-book revolution may ultimately evolve into a commercial market, where people rent e-books largely from for-profit companies (either for free as part of promotional efforts, for a small fee, or under an Amazon-type subscriber service that includes many other features and benefits in addition to e-book rentals). Such a trend could squeeze libraries out of the digital book market, at least for nonacademic books and bestsellers. The authors of viewpoints in this chapter discuss whether libraries should be able to buy and lend e-books.

There Should Be a Vibrant Rental of E-books by Libraries

Martin Taylor

Martin Taylor is a publisher and consultant with an interest in information technology, the Internet, and business media. He writes an online blog called eReport about ebooks and digital publishing.

One of the big issues looming on the digital horizon is the role libraries will play with ebooks. A pre-emptive move last month by the UK [United Kingdom] government has up-set booksellers and shows that the industry here, too, needs to get involved in this debate.

The UK Solution

So far, libraries' digital activity has mostly been confined to research uses. The prevalence of the cumbersome PC as the main reading platform means the bread and butter of the book trade, fiction and general non-fiction, has barely been touched. But mobile reading devices and a surge in availability of popular ebooks are pushing libraries into the digital mainstream.

The few libraries experimenting today with ebook downloads typically have very thin collections. This is partly due to tight budgets but also stems from concerns by publishers and authors about how—indeed whether—libraries should lend digital editions of their books.

It's the latter that has prompted the UK government to legislate so that patrons in libraries can download digital editions to their ebook readers without libraries infringing copyright. At the same time, it will issue an order under legislation "preventing libraries from charging for ebooks lending of any sort, including remotely."

On the face of it, this looks like a big win for the reading public. Most people I speak to about ebooks get excited by the idea that they'll be able to borrow them free from their libraries. And most people have a visceral sense that borrowing from a public library should be free to all. But this excitement is not shared as acutely by publishers, authors and booksellers.

[Book publisher] Macmillan US CEO [chief executive officer] John Sargent put the industry problem succinctly when he said recently, "In the past, getting a book from libraries has had a tremendous amount of friction. You have to go to the library, maybe the book has been checked out and you have to come back another time ... With ebooks, you sit on your couch in your living room and go to the library website, see if the library has it ... You get the book, read it, return it and get another, all without paying a thing ... How is that a good model for us?"

For much of the public, politicians, and librarians, this seems like a perfectly good model which accords with the common view that the digital world should operate the same way as print. But it is likely to be bad news for publishers, authors and booksellers. The former might lose sales because libraries can lend ebooks more efficiently (they need fewer websites than physical libraries) and they don't wear out or get lost. And publishers, authors and booksellers all potentially suffer if the free option is as "frictionless" to get as their more expensive paid editions. And there might be less desire to "own" an electronic file than a real book.

Perversely, libraries are likely to suffer too from the UK government mandate to lend all ebooks free of charge. Most will not be able to afford a serious ebook lending programme without painful cuts to other services. If no other measures are taken, the result will be a crippled ebook service with a very limited selection. Ironically, booksellers concerned about competing with free loans should probably cheer the unintended consequence of this heavy-handed move.

But let's not cheer too soon. Faced with this outcome, the government might tip the balance in libraries' favour by forcing rightsholders to make big concessions, effectively subsidising libraries and setting up an even stronger competitor for booksellers. Its planned copyright changes to let libraries lend ebooks with or without publisher permission shows it's not averse to forcing rightsholders' hands.

Ebooks need a range of channels and price points too, to properly service the market and maximise the value of our creative assets.

A Range of Channels and Price Points

So what is a reasonable role for libraries and how do we achieve this balance of interests? To avoid the heavy-handed legislative approach we're seeing unfold in the UK, we need to talk directly to the library sector and other stakeholders in our own part of the world.

And we need to consider how the ebooks ecosystem will evolve.

If we look at the film industry as a comparison, there's an initial cinematic release followed by release to rental and sell-through channels, then pay TV, then free-to-air TV. Through this measured roll-out, the industry manages to extract value at every price point, including free and sells through many channels to reach as much of the market as possible. About 80% of the film industry's income is earned after cinematic release.

Ebooks need a range of channels and price points too, to properly service the market and maximise the value of our creative assets. And with books it's not just an economic equation: we have to consider social impacts.

So which channels will open up for ebooks? We're in the early stages of developing a "full price" channel and still have a lot of work to do selling the value of digital books to consumers. And we can expect that libraries will offer some sort of free channel, whether selectively or open to all. Other (legal) free-to-consumer channels might emerge, perhaps through ISPs [Internet service providers]—and might have to develop to stem piracy.

I personally would like to see a vibrant rental channel for ebooks. And I'd like to see both libraries and booksellers participating, perhaps with release dates delayed just as DVDs today follow cinematic release. This would be an interesting "back to the future" scenario for booksellers. Before the public library movement, they had a thriving book rental market and in their heyday, there were more than 1000 "circulating libraries" in mid-nineteenth century Britain.

A paid rental option could bring much-needed money into libraries' strained coffers, resulting in a better service to patrons who can pay and, with this improved funding, a better free service for those who can't. For publishers and authors, it offers the prospect of fair compensation for readership through libraries.

While booksellers might be concerned that libraries are straying into commercial territory, it will be worse all around if they are backed into a corner by politicians and a public with high expectations, while not given the resources to deliver on these aspirations.

We'd then confront two equally grim scenarios: a high quality free service competing aggressively with booksellers and largely paid for by onerous terms thrust on publishers and authors by legislation. Or a crippled public library service struggling with dwindling patronage and increasing irrelevance.

These are tough issues with far-reaching impacts. Time to start talking and find a way through this.

The E-book Market Must Open to Facilitate E-book Usage by Libraries

Tim Kambitsch

Tim Kambitsch, executive director of the Dayton Metro Library in Ohio, is especially interested in information technology.

It is fashionable to declare Digital Rights Management (DRM) [technologies used to limit access to copyrighted materials] dead. And maybe in the world of music it is. For eBooks in the library marketplace, however, DRM is alive and well. The book publishers who may be more conservative than the music industry in trying to protect their intellectual property are willing to stymie sales in electronic formats to maximize their sense of security.

In the ideal open-yet-market-driven eBook environment there won't be DRM, but regardless of whether DRM lives on, the closed vertically integrated world of eBooks sales to libraries presents a bigger problem; it is that environment that needs to change. For libraries to both offer electronic collections and maintain their role of building collections for the long term we need a layered environment where the purchase of materials is separated from where those purchased materials are hosted. Further, library patrons deserve distinct choices for the programs and devices they use for readings.

E-books Buying

"Purchasing" eBooks may be overstating the actual relationship to the materials we select and offer our patrons. The concept that libraries buy-to-own eBooks is more conceptual than factual. We select titles; we pay different prices for titles that seem to have a relationship to the hardcopy price of the title. However, marketing materials and licenses agreements we sign don't give one that warm and fuzzy feeling. It might be better to refer to these as titles we have licensed access for our patrons.

Libraries should be able to select eBook vendors in an open environment, separate from other considerations such as where those titles are hosted and how patrons might access them.

Libraries spending upward and beyond $100,000 per year for these collections and the cumulative investment in eBooks and downloadable audio books with our vendors may only last as long as the vendor stays in business and as long as we are willing and able to pay the annual hosting fees of that vendor. With that being the case vendors are building a captive environment, making it difficult if not impossible for us to walk away from.

Libraries should be able to select eBook vendors in an open environment, separate from other considerations such as where those titles are hosted and how patrons might access them. In an open environment libraries might buy books directly from individual authors or publishers, but more likely from brokers such as Overdrive, B&T and Ebsco. Libraries should find these vendors competing for my business by offering low prices but also by offering better tools to aid in the acquisition, cataloging and management of digital content. We should be able to buy my eBooks from one or all of these sources.

The one title per simultaneous user model is something [with which] the publishers feel comfortable, particularly with the most popular titles. This model is a strong carry over from the hard copy world and may be difficult for publishers to deviate from when granting licenses. However, other options should be available. Similar to rental collections, licenses for selected copies of best sellers might be limited to only a six month period. They get loaned out just like those that are licensed indefinitely, but the library will pay marginally less to have access to them for just six months. Naturally the hosting servers will know when those copies expire and adjust the number of copies available to a library's patrons as the rental copies expire.

Hosting E-books for Posterity

In licensing books a library has the responsibility to ensure that for titles it selects it will ensure that appropriate restrictions (i.c. DRM) are in place. We currently rely on our vendors to provide the secure environment so to meet our licensing agreements with the IP [intellectual property] owners. There is a real convenience to that. However libraries may have greater needs to take ownership of that responsibility. In a truly open environment libraries should be able to make choices of which vendor(s) are chosen to host eBook titles and collections independent of which vendors from which I choose to buy content. With the library taking responsibility for copyright and license enforcement, the library also has flexibility:

- The library chooses which vendor will host its e-content. This might be a locally managed host or it might be a host operated by a consortium of libraries. The library might also choose a single vendor to host their eBook collections. Overdrive, Ebsco, OCLC, B&T and maybe even Amazon or Google might compete to host my collection.

- The library could elect to move that content from one vendor's server to another as it see[s] fit in the best interest of its patrons as long as it operates within the original restrictions of the license agreement with the IP owner.

- Most importantly, by taking ownership of the decision of where and how to host all of its eBooks, the library has a better chance of integrating the various collections it has chosen to license from individual authors, publishers and brokers. Currently eBooks from one vendor are intellectually organized in a completely different context from that of other vendors. When the mechanics of downloading of materials differ we are creating unacceptable confusion on the part of library users.

Within the server software the file format it produces would be decided upon request of the client hardware/ software.

Freeing Our Patrons

For libraries to compete with Amazon, Barnes and Noble, Google and other eBook stores they must offer the best possible user experience to their patrons. We can help achieve this by offering the end user a level playing field when it comes to e-readers. Additionally libraries shouldn't be penalized for offering choices of formats for the same title.

Library patrons should have choices of eBook reader hardware and software. As users check out copies from the library the eBook server should automatically offer them the format they want. Libraries should never have to make a priori decisions to buy x number of copies in one format and x number of copies in another format from the same vendor. We had to do it with DVDs vs. videotape copies, and with large print vs. standard print copies, but with digital content this should not be necessary.

Within the server software the file format it produces would be decided upon request of the client hardware/ software. As users check out a copy of a title, they (or their client hardware/software preferences) will select the format and an appropriate DRM for that device. It would be applied on the fly. Never again should a patron see an available copy encoded for a specific format sit on the electronic book shelf while all available copies for their device are checked out. The mix of formats checked out to patrons might change from day to day, but the hosting server would ensure the total copies on loan would not exceed what is licensed.

Library patrons shouldn't be forced to use just the client e-reader provided by the hosting service. In fact, as e-readers devices become more intelligent, users may have many different choices. Today ePub-formatted books hosted by Overdrive can be opened by Adobe's Digital Editions and by Overdrive's iOS and Android Media Console clients. But other client software exists. BlueFire is an example. Seeing such choices emerge is a step in the right direction, but currently it takes a pretty sophisticated user to elect alternative clients. Selecting a different client should be as simple as selecting from a dialog box. For instance, as long as the original licensing and DRM requirements are satisfied, then a patron could choose one client for daytime reading and another for nighttime reading—even on the same device.

New yet-to-be-developed public domain or commercial clients that integrate an e-reader with social networking features such as Facebook and Twitter updates might be the preferred client by some, while consistency with previously purchased eBooks might make it a better choice for other library patrons.

Moving Forward

The current vendors in the library eBook marketplace may cringe at some of the above suggestions. They may see profits erode as they are forced to compete more aggressively where they haven't had to before. However, these recommendations are not offered to drive them out of business. Publishers may have to charge more per title if libraries will never have to buy replacement copies. They may also have to pay more per title if they buy fewer copies because they don't have to buy different versions just to accommodate the odd eBook reader. Hosting fees may have to rise substantially if a library wants a vendor to host all of their eBooks not just the eBooks they buy from that vendor. Individual library patrons may actually want to pay for a superior e-reader client or [they] may choose to make do with a free or shareware reader. Certainly how various players make money may change but ultimately more eBooks will be purchased and more revenues and profits will ensue.

Libraries want book authors, publishers, and brokers to succeed. If they cannot make appropriate revenues libraries won't have an opportunity to offer eBooks to their patrons. Opening up each segment of this market to competition will foster better products, better support and a better user experience. Libraries will probably have to pay more, but their collections will be better integrated into their service model and libraries will have a longer more secure future for the collections they are investing in today.

E-book Sellers Should Listen to the Concerns of Libraries

Kate Sheehan

Kate Sheehan is a blogger and the open source implementation coordinator for Bibliomation, a consortium of public and school libraries in Connecticut.

On February 28 [2011], the library e-book vendor Overdrive announced that one publisher's e-books would expire from library collections after 26 circulations, and the publisher in question was challenging longstanding library resource sharing and group purchasing practices. Within hours, the publisher was identified as HarperCollins, and Twitter, Facebook, and the biblioblogosphere exploded with posts trailing the hashtag #hcod for HarperCollins/Overdrive.

Many librarians are joining a boycott of HarperCollins, even though boycotting doesn't come naturally to librarians. Our professional instincts drive us to share content, not limit access to it based on our interests. But this isn't just about library interests. It isn't even about traditional boycotting.

Libraries' Concerns

We are not going to bring HarperCollins to its knees with a boycott, nor do we want to. But libraries are heavily invested in publishing and publishers. Like everyone else in the book world, librarians have been trying to figure out our place in an e-book marketplace. Unlike large booksellers, we don't have the means to engineer a customized solution.

Librarians don't begrudge our for-profit partners their income. We work with booksellers, and we want publishers and authors to be profitable. We introduce readers to new authors and titles, we support book groups, and we spearhead communitywide reads.

Libraries are one of the last true commons in modern life, celebrating and championing the right to read and freedom of access to information. Stewardship of the written record is integral to our mission. Libraries don't have a financial stake in the publishing business so much as society has a cultural stake in the future of libraries.

Many librarians have expressed a strong interest in tiered plans, with options for cheaper, expiring e-books.

Financially, libraries are beholden to their members, not to a profit margin. Librarians have to be able to tell patrons that we've been responsible stewards of their money. We can't do that with HarperCollins's plan, not just because we can't afford it now, but because we can't sustain it going forward. Not every library offers e-books yet, and those that do would like to expand their offerings. If HarperCollins sets the bar for other publishers, libraries will be unable to start or grow their e-book collections.

Currently, librarians rely on the First Sale doctrine—which makes it legal to circulate materials we purchase and manage—along with our trustworthiness. We enforce copyright laws as much as we can, teaching our patrons about fair use and piracy. We haven't been Xeroxing print books in our back rooms, and we're not about to start teaching people to torrent. If publishers are worried about e-book piracy, librarians are ready and willing allies.

Many libraries lease print books to keep costs down and their patrons happy, but those leasing agreements are equitable for everyone. Publishers, authors, librarians, and readers all benefit from book rentals without damaging our long-term investment in the commons. We struggle with the indefinite shelf life of e-books just as publishers do. Most libraries don't want to own 20 or 30 copies of every bestseller in perpetuity. Many librarians have expressed a strong interest in tiered plans, with options for cheaper, expiring e-books.

Another troubling aspect of the HarperCollins message is the attempt to prevent resource sharing, which is a core value for librarians. Reciprocal borrowing agreements and interlibrary loan mean that even the tiniest library can offer its patrons the world. Consortial Overdrive plans allow smaller libraries to get in on the e-book action. However, neither resource sharing nor group purchasing means we're giving away the store. Librarians diligently enforce agreements with vendors, and the implication that we are not careful in granting membership stings.

The boycott of HarperCollins is not a knee-jerk reaction to feeling slighted. It is a demand to have our voices heard and to protect our already-squeezed budgets until a solution that benefits readers, libraries, and publishers can be found. I'm glad a publisher is willing to experiment with a new model for e-book circulation in libraries, though my hope is that HarperCollins will blaze a trail for collaboration with libraries, not undermine the doctrine that enables us to serve our communities. Publishers, it is not your responsibility to keep libraries afloat. But should it be your mission to close them down?

Both Libraries and Book Publishers Should Respond Creatively to the Public Demand for E-books

Kent Anderson

Kent Anderson is the chief executive officer (CEO) and publisher of the Journal of Bone & Joint Surgery, *a medical publication.*

If you ever wanted evidence that supply and demand aren't the only forces in the economic game, now you have it. There may be an invisible hand, but there's now a visible hand, and it's throttling things back in the case of libraries and e-books. The visible hand is the hand of publishers, and its goal is to slow the transition to e-books so that profit margins remain as robust as possible and the transition to e-reading remains manageable. Even as they do so, Amazon is being accused of being "predatory," turning publishers' knuckles white as they hold on for the ride.

Demand is outstripping supply in a world where supply should be endless. Adding insult to injury, librarians have one of their icons signing on with Amazon.com to curate sets of rescued book titles. And while publishers and librarians are both worried about what all this might mean for them, a unifying middle ground is hard to find.

Abundance and Scarcity

An acute pressure point is that e-book demand has surged after the 2011 holidays, when millions of new e-readers were switched on. Immediately, libraries lending e-books fell behind, as a recent story in the *Washington Post* details:

Want to take out the new John Grisham? Get in line. As of Friday morning, 288 people were ahead of you in the Fairfax County Public Library system, waiting for one of 43 copies. You'd be the 268th person waiting for *The Girl with the Dragon Tattoo*, with 47 copies. And the Steve Jobs biography? Forget it. The publisher, Simon & Schuster, doesn't make any of its digital titles available to libraries. Frustration is building on all sides: among borrowers who can't get what they want when they want it; among librarians trying to stock their virtual shelves and working with limited budgets and little cooperation from some publishers; and among publishers who are fearful of piracy and wading into a digital future that could further destabilize their industry. In many cases, the publishers are limiting the number of e-books made available to libraries.

The ALA [American Library Association] is attempting to address these emerging problems by meeting with the top executives at Macmillan, Simon & Schuster, and Penguin later this month [January 2012].

Publishers are nervous. Libraries are frustrated. Amazon has become a publisher and a major third-party for e-book checkouts at libraries. Apple has announced a textbook program. Google Books is far from dead.

The reliable contrast between abundance and scarcity is at the heart of the problem facing book publishers and libraries working their traditional exchanges.

Abundance creates one of the perceptual challenges for all involved—the perception that electronic resources are much cheaper and more abundant than physical items. In the age of scarcity, a publisher could sell one copy of *The Girl with the Dragon Tattoo* to a local library, and patrons would have understood what they're competing for—a definite physical object that isn't at the library when it's checked out. Allow three e-book copies to be on deposit, and suddenly waiting for a copy seems odd. Out of the frustration this creates, pirating a copy seems a rational response.

Traditional publishers with their value chains and libraries with their place in the value chain are vulnerable. As Trey Ratcliff writes:

> It turns out that tech companies—especially Apple and Amazon—are the new publishers. And this is, of course, because their technology disintermediates all the component steps required for a physical book. We have all seen the numbers about the growth of e-books and how every category is impinging on the traditional book categories.

Given the impressive profit margins of e-books, the ability for authors to sell a short book at a decent price (no demands for heft-making filler!), and marketing that works like magic with social media, e-books are allowing authors to move out of or avoid entirely traditional publishing houses, all while requiring less traditional editing and production work and selling in new ways—in short, a new value chain is emerging, the true sign of disruption. Books are being made, but in a new way, and with new players.

Libraries Should Get Out of the E-book Business

Bobbi Newman

Bobbi Newman is a librarian, speaker, and writer in the Des Moines, Iowa, area, as well as a blogger at Librarian by Day, a website that focuses on issues affecting libraries and librarians.

Should Libraries Get Out of the eBook Business? Or get out at least until there is a better system?

I know what you are going to say, I can hear it already—"We can't! Our patrons demand ebooks!" Except the truth is our patrons want a lot of things we can't give them—to always be first on the waiting list for the new James Patterson, to not pay fines when their books are late, for the library to be open earlier or later, or to have a system besides Dewey because despite using it their entire lives they still cannot figure it out. When it comes to ebooks, we cannot give them what they want, not really, we cannot give them books from Simon and Schuster or Macmillan or new books from Penguin or Hachette, and not more than 26 times from HarperCollins, and probably not many books from Random House. What we can do, what maybe we should do, is spend their tax money wisely, and I am no longer convinced that spending it on the current ebook system is a wise move.

The Demand

First let's look at the demand. As librarians we spend a great deal of time thinking and talking about books and subsequently ebooks. But the truth is we spend far more time focusing on ebooks than the population. Reports vary on the actual percentage of the population that actually owns an ereader but general consensus agrees that after the holiday season this year [December 2011] it is only about 19 percent of the population that owns an ereader, if you factor in tablets that number rises to 29%. Of course there is no guarantee that those tablet owners are reading ebooks on their device, but I'll be generous and go with 29%. Ok, you say but we still have to serve that 29%.

We are in the midst of the ebook wars.

The Supply

But what are we serving them? One only has to look at *Library Journal*'s "A Guide to Publishers in the Library Ebook Market" to realize it's pretty slim pickings. So we're providing a mediocre access at best.

The Process

Plus if you have the fortune to be the person at your library who is responsible for helping patrons with ebooks and troubleshooting problems you know that the process is a nightmare. In order to borrow library ebooks patrons must have a compatible device, a home computer capable of running Adobe Digital Editions, a high-speed internet connection, and enough tech savvy to set everything up and get it to work correctly. If all goes well, wonderful! But if one thing goes wrong, woe to the librarian providing support over the phone. Honestly the process is a nightmare. The most beautiful thing to happen to the ebook lending process was the partnership with Amazon that allowed it to happen wirelessly.

A Mess

The whole thing is a hot mess. A hot mess that is consuming our time, our resources and our money. We are in the midst of the ebook wars, just look at the number of proprietary systems and file formats.

Or look at the regular headlines about publishers fighting with Amazon over pricing, the latest being Amazon yanks 5,000 titles from Independent Publishers Group, a Chicago book distributor.

I can't help but wonder if [writer] Guy LeCharles Gonzales is right when he writes:

> Stop buying ebooks across the board, at any price, under any terms. Let publishers fight it out with Amazon, and when the dust finally settles (it will) and a viable business model appears (maybe), begin negotiating anew, on solid ground, with whomever's left standing.
>
> In the meantime, libraries can redirect those precious resources and finances being flagged for ebooks towards more tangible initiatives in their respective communities.
>
> Surely every library has a service gap or three to fill that's more valuable than overpaying for temporary licenses to files and platforms they don't own, that may or may not work on their patrons' devices of choice, and whose pricing can fluctuate more wildly than that of crude oil and Netflix stock.

Maybe libraries should just stop buying ebooks until there is a real, viable solution to the situation. Do not mistake me, I do not think we should stop looking for a solution or stop advocating on behalf of our patrons, but I do think perhaps we should stop throwing good money at a bad solution.

I am certainly not the only one thinking about this, [libraran] Andy Woodworth offers a list of alternative uses for your ebook budgets. . . .

We need a solution to the library/ebook problem, we need a seat at the table in ebook discussions, but right now libraries (and our patrons) are just collateral damage in the ebooks war.

[Blogger] Karen Schneider points out in her recent post about publishers, ebooks, and libraries:

Note that publishers have had their eyes on libraries for a long time. A pioneering librarian, Marvin Scilken, led the charge to expose imbalance in bookstore/library pricing decades ago, which resulted in an agreement on library pricing that no doubt has stuck in publishers' craws ever since. Depending on who is in office, there would have to be some similar sympathy these days. Studying those hearings and their arguments might be useful.

How Marvin proceeded, and succeeded, might be a very useful research question to pursue in the ALA [American Library Association] library and ALA archives—and could be a great class project for that class I don't have time to teach. But one thing's for sure: the good work Marvin did in 1966 is now being upended. Then again, maybe, in its own way, it can be repeated.

I have been thinking for a while now that we will not find a solution by politely saying "please, sir, I want some more". After all we (as a society, not libraries) did not get the first sale doctrine out of the goodness of someone's heart, it came from a court case. Maybe we need to stop asking. It wouldn't be the first time.

There Are Good Reasons for Libraries Not to Use E-books Yet

Evan Williamson

Evan Williamson is a librarian in the Jackson, Mississippi, area and a blogger at Banned Library, a website that focuses on books and library issues.

Oh, what a lovely tea party this ebook experience is, am I right? With prices constantly shifting, publishers competing, and the overall industry flopping over to a new way of reading, who would not get stuck in this mire? Well, here I come to offer up a little round of thoughts I like to call "Screw'em." Libraries are a foundation in the community. For at least 100 years, the library has been a fixture in almost every city and town across America. The library to the community is a point of civilization, as a bookshelf is to a home. Think about a home without a bookshelf: an empty dwelling with one bare, hanging light and from one corner of that dank room, small cries are heard. You do not want to go into that house.

The library represents the willingness of a community to not only think for itself but also to grow by allowing free representation of ideas and information. By taking away the danger aspect of "being left behind," libraries should really review the following . . . reasons they should not use ebooks yet:

1. *Most libraries will not have the tech support to handle every device.*

Ebooks are still a relatively new field. When the Internet gained popularity and libraries with the money began getting computers, sure there were some hang ups. But I bet you dollars to doughnut-holes all those computers had only one operating system (Windows or Mac) that by week two most of the staff had a handle on enough to teach every yokel that came in how to get an AOL email. There were even books to teach you, most of them pointedly describing their readers as "dummies" and "idiots." But look at the landscape of ereaders. Every version of every device has its own features and whats-a-doodles, and let's not even get into the formats. To expect every patron with every device to be serviced just as they are with the library website and books is absurd because every ereader is not created equally.

Digital content can be a huge money maker as long as you tighten the reins to the breaking point.

---

2. *Most libraries will not have the tech to support the service.*

Does your library have a website? Good. Does your library host your website? *Host.* It means you have a big computer that your website lives in. Ah, you pay for that from somebody else? Well, that's what you are going to have to do with ebooks then. Not all but a lot of libraries do not have full time tech support and often pay proprietary companies to handle all that for them. We handle the search coding, link it to your in-house system, bada-bing-bada-boom you got yourself a library website. Not so with ebooks. You will almost certainly have to pay someone else, like Overdrive, to hold on to all those little files that will be accessed by your patrons. That leads us to the next point:

3. *The ebook industry is constantly changing.*

I know, I know, it will always be changing, publishing took decades to get to a stable place, I got a paper cut. Yeah, I know all that. But ebooks just became really profitable. What Harper Collins has just taught us is that the industry wants a piece of that sweet, sweet action and they do not want folks to give it away for free. Think about it, once they sold you a pbook (paper book) you could give it to a friend, throw it away, hell, use it to light a Thanksgiving parade mascot on fire, they already had your money. But what they learned from Napster over a decade ago is that digital content can be a huge money maker as long as you tighten the reins to the breaking point and never, never let the college kids get a hold on it.

4. *The patrons that use ereaders the most use the library the least.*

Think of all your swanky non-library friends and their fancy ereaders. Try to recall the last time you saw them in a library beyond the odd function or two. There may be an exception that proves the rule, but not by a long shot. People who can afford ereaders and are knowledgeable enough to use them have no use for the library once they are out of college. They do not use library services out of spite or anything, not most of them anyway, they just have no need because their home Internet connection and ability to spend a few bucks on an instant download override a trip to the library, either for information or entertainment.

Many Libraries Cannot Afford E-book Prices

Michael Kelley

Michael Kelley is news editor for Library Journal, *a trade publication for librarians.*

New prices for Random House's ebooks took effect on Thursday [March 1, 2012], and as the details emerged a number of librarians across the country expressed dismay at the doubling and tripling in prices they are seeing.

"We're very concerned. These are tough times for libraries. It's very tough here in Louisville," said Debbe Oberhausen, manager of collection services, at the Louisville Free Public Library [Kentucky]. "We want to provide this service, but this kind of pricing is really going to take a huge chunk of our budget," she said.

On Wednesday, Oberhausen bought *Eisenhower in War and Peace* by Jean Edward Smith for $40 via OverDrive. On Thursday, the price was $120. The print version of the book, with the library's discount, is a little over $20 (it retails at $40). For *Blessings* by Anna Quindlen the ebook price went from $15 to $45.

"We're happy they are continuing to sell to libraries, very happy," Oberhausen said. "But this price increase is really, really hard," she said.

Random House's Policy

Random House, which first announced the price hike (without details) on February 2 when it reaffirmed its commitment to the library ebook market, provided the following breakdown for what it is now charging library ebook distributors:

- Titles available in print as new hardcovers: $65–$85

- Titles available for several months, or generally timed to paperback release: $25–$50

- New children's titles available in print as hardcovers: $35–$85

- Older children's titles and children's paperbacks: $25–$45

"We believe our new library e-pricing reflects the high value placed on perpetuity of lending and simultaneity of availability for our titles," said Stuart Applebaum, a Random House spokesperson. "Understandably, every library will have its own perspective on this topic, and we are prepared to listen, learn, and adapt as appropriate," he said.

"Simultaneity" here means that Random House's titles are available to libraries on the same date the retail edition is put on sale. It is not referring to simultaneous, multiple user access. The model remains one book, one user.

Applebaum said that the publishing house, which is the only one of the Big Six [book publishers] to make its ebooks available without restriction for library lending, is setting the library ebook price with "far less definitive, encompassing circulation data" than the sell-through information used to determine retail pricing.

"We are requesting data that libraries can share about their patrons' borrowing patterns that over time will better enable us to establish mutually workable pricing levels that will best serve the overall e-book ecosystem," Applebaum said.

LJ's [*Library Journal*'s] 2012 Book Buying Survey showed a 102 percent jump in ebook circulation, and 74 percent of the ebook patrons in *LJ*'s Patron Profiles report say they want even more ebooks in the library.

Applebaum said the new pricing does not affect Random House titles already in a library's collection.

Random House's increase was to distributors, such as OverDrive, which in turn can add its own increase on to what libraries ultimately pay. OverDrive, by far the largest distributor of ebooks to public libraries, declined to comment, but a number of librarians told *LJ* that the company holds closely information about its own markups.

Frustrations of Libraries

The rationale for the price hike to distributors was to align ebook pricing with Random House's Books on Tape audio book downloads for library lending.

[Random House has] tripled their prices on every title. A book that a week ago we purchased for $28.00 now costs $84.00.

"They're aligning it with the e-audio version as a library edition price," said Christopher Platt, the deputy director, collections and circulating operations, for the New York Public Library. "It would affect the number of units we acquire, but we're not freaking out about it. They're still in libraries after all," he said.

Others also said they will have to rethink their collection decisions.

"They've tripled their prices on every title. A book that a week ago we purchased for $28.00 now costs $84.00," said Scarlett Fisher-Herreman, the technical services & collection development supervisor, at the Topeka and Shawnee County Public Library in Kansas, whose director, Gina Millsap, is seeking the presidency of the American Library Association. "I looked back at Random House titles we've purchased since December and looked up a number of titles, both new and titles they've had for years on Overdrive. Everything has tripled in price: kids, YA [young adult], adult, fiction, and nonfiction," she said.

Fisher-Herreman, who had been bracing for an increase in the 50 percent range, said she found the tripling of price frustrating and surprising. For example, *The 10 Easter Egg Hunters*, a children's title by Janet Schulman, was affordable at $8.99, but it now costs $26.97.

"We simply can't afford to pay three times the price for the same titles. I will be working with my collection development team to determine how we move forward now that we know the severity of the price increase," Fisher-Herreman said.

At the North Texas Library Partners, Carolyn Brewer, the executive director, had her staff make a duplicate cart of a Random House order the library had just recently placed. She found a 200 percent increase was the norm, with some titles hitting the 300 percent mark.

"I'm worried that, between the lack of content available and the new pricing structures, we won't be able to meet the demand for popular materials," Brewer said.

Trent Garcia, the electronic resources librarian at the San Francisco Public Library, also felt a bit nonplussed: glad that Random House was still in the market but concerned about "a pretty steep increase."

"The impact I foresee is we won't be able to purchase as many titles as we were before," Garcia said. "And in terms of our holds ratio, how many additional copies we will be able to buy will probably be affected as well," he said.

The holds on ebooks are already notoriously long in libraries across the country.

Kathy Petlewski, the electronic resources librarian at the Plymouth District Library in Plymouth, Michigan, wrote on her blog on Thursday after seeing the price increases:

The first thing that popped into my mind was that Random House must really hate libraries. Perhaps this isn't true, but it will take a lot of convincing for me to believe otherwise. Do they not realize that libraries are hard hit by the economic downturn and that our budgets are shrinking. How do they think we can afford to build a decent collection of e-books when we're spending over $100 per book? I am terribly disappointed by this latest turn of events.

Applebaum said the company remained committed to serving libraries.

"Throughout our long history of mutual respect and partnership with libraries we have endeavored to satisfy our shared goals," Applebaum said. "We are certain our ongoing straightforward dialogues with them on library e-lending will continue to yield constructive results," he said.

CHAPTER 3

How Should E-books Be Priced?

Chapter Preface

As the demand for e-books has soared, publishers and book retailers have struggled to determine how e-books should be priced for sale. Initially, the giant online book retailer Amazon, which also manufactures the popular e-book reader, the Kindle, led the market in e-book sales by buying e-books from publishers at wholesale prices and then selling them cheaply, sometimes for less than Amazon's cost. Typically, Amazon priced popular e-books at about $9.99 and many self-published e-books at only 99 cents. Amazon's pricing, though popular with consumers, rankled publishers and led to an e-book pricing war as other players such as iPad-maker Apple also began to sell e-books through its online iBook store. Apple's efforts to undercut Amazon, in turn, brought the US government into the mix, because of suspicion that Apple and book publishers were colluding to keep e-book prices high.

Amazon's business plan involves pricing e-books lower than paper books in order to stimulate sales of its Kindle e-reader. It hopes to dominate the e-book market by keeping the prices of both the Kindle and its e-books competitive compared to the prices charged by other e-reader/tablet makers and booksellers. E-book publishers, by contrast, want to protect the main part of their business (hardback and paperback books) by making sure that e-book prices do not drop too low. Also, publishers want to protect their profit margins on e-books. Even though e-books cost publishers less to produce, because there are no printing costs, publishers argue that e-books still require publishers to pay for many of the same editing and marketing services required to publish paper books.

However, when publishers have pressed Amazon to raise its e-book prices above $9.99, Amazon has responded by dropping those publishers' books from its online bookstore. In 2010, for example, when Macmillan asked Amazon to increase its e-book prices to about $15, Amazon temporarily delisted Macmillan books from its website. Amazon used the same tactic in 2012 against another publisher, the Independent Publishers' Group (IPG), after it refused to grant Amazon deep discounts on its e-books. Amazon has fought in other ways also to maintain its low-price leadership position against competitor booksellers. When Google launched a new online service called Google Play, which included a week of 25-cent deals on certain e-book titles, Amazon quietly matched Google prices.

In 2011, chief executive officer of Apple, Steve Jobs, sought to challenge Amazon's domination of the e-book market by making deals with major book publishers. In 2010, Apple planned to introduce its first iPad and start its own iBook store but did not want to get into a direct price war with Amazon. Instead, the company negotiated an agreement with publishers for them to sell e-books to Apple priced according to what is called the agency model. Under this pricing model, the book publishers can set whatever price they want for e-books, and Apple gets 30 percent of that price. Importantly, part of the deal was that publishers can no longer use the wholesale pricing model with other retailers (such as Amazon), and if other retailers continued to price e-books lower than Apple, Apple could match those prices. This Apple strategy basically leveled the playing field for all retailers, while giving publishers the right to set higher prices for e-books. Publishers were thrilled with this result, but consumers were not happy because they feared that allowing publishers to set prices would mean that e-book prices would rise.

This potential impact on consumers caught the attention of the US Justice Department (DOJ), and it began investigating the Apple deal with publishers and threatening to file an antitrust lawsuit against them for colluding to raise the price of e-books. The five major publishers investigated, along with Apple, were Simon & Schuster, Macmillan, HarperCollins, Hachette Book Group, and Penguin Group. The parties began settlement negotiations. The publishers denied acting jointly to raise prices, arguing that their embrace of agency pricing actually enhanced competition by preventing Amazon from gaining a monopoly in the e-book market. The price of many e-books from big publishers is still actually higher than the printed versions (which are not subject to the agency pricing model). The result is that three of the publishers—HarperCollins, Simon & Schuster, and Hachette Book Group—agreed to settle with the Justice Department, but the DOJ on April 11, 2012, sued Apple and the remaining two publishers, alleging a conspiracy to inflate e-book prices and limit competition.

Various solutions to the overall problem of e-book pricing have been considered. One proposal is to preserve the agency pricing but allow publishers to delay the publication of e-books following the release of the hardcover version. A similar policy is used by movie producers, who delay the release of DVDs for a period of time after movies are released to theaters. As of 2012, the outcome of this debate was still unknown, but many observers expect the e-book market to continue to grow as sales of printed books were anticipated to continue declining. The authors of the viewpoints in this chapter present different views about pricing in the e-book market.

E-book Pricing Should Be Decided by E-book Publishers

TendersInfo News

TendersInfo News is the leading business opportunity platform and information services company, providing the latest up-to-date information.

I can't believe I'm going to say this, but Amazon needs to stop meddling in e-book pricing and let the free market do its thing. Over the past few days, a major skirmish in the e-book pricing wars erupted between Amazon and book publisher Macmillan. After a nearly yearlong dispute over electronic book edition pricing, Amazon stopped all sales of Macmillan titles, even print copies, in a pretty shocking display of brinksmanship.

The E-book Pricing War

Macmillan responded with a full-page ad detailing the fight with Amazon and its hoped-for pricing model. And finally, Amazon released a statement saying it was capitulating to Macmillan's demands and selling the books "even at prices we believe are needlessly high for e-books."

Now, before I go any further, let me clarify one thing: I absolutely believe $15 is too high a price for e-books. I believe and have said many times that the publishing industry threatens to strangle the baby e-book market in its crib with everything from DRM [Digital Rights Managment: technology that prevents an e-book from being copied] to refusing to allow text-to-speech features in e-readers to trying to impose antiquated release windows for e-book editions, and that includes the idea that a digital copy of a book should cost $15. That said, it's time to let the market decide what it's willing to pay. Amazon is, finally, doing the right thing (albeit passive-aggressively in the extreme) by getting out of the way of publisher pricing and letting consumers decide what they'll pay for e-books. What Macmillan is asking for is the same thing the music industry eventually demanded from both Apple and Amazon: variable pricing for digital goods. Yes, Macmillan wants to price new and major titles between $12.99 and $14.99, but they're also talking about a pricing floor of $5.99. They're trying to maximize revenue on the top sellers, but also retain the flexibility to drop the prices as the market demands. That's actually how it should work.

The Perfect Balance

Now, you could argue that Apple launched digital music sales into the stratosphere by turning digital music into a loss leader with the 99-cent track. But in truth, we had no idea what the market was willing to pay for digital songs. That consumers snapped up those 99-cent tracks could be proof that the price was too low. The variable pricing scheme may not be as popular with buyers, but it is generating revenue for the labels, and business is all about finding that perfect balance of sales and revenue. In the digital music world, labels are testing the price elasticity of demand for their product in the reverse order it normally happens. Starting low and raising prices over time is, higher revenues notwithstanding, not the standard way of things.

E-book Consumers Prefer Amazon's Low E-book Prices

Charles Cooper

Charles Cooper is an executive editor at CNET News, a technology news producer. Previously, he covered technology and business issues as a reporter and blogger for various news organizations, including CBSNews.com.

Remember how much money e-readers were supposed to save book buyers? It was among the big reasons why 20 million Americans decided to take the plunge.

So why is it that consumers are still paying through the nose for e-book titles that ought to cost a fraction of the price charged for the used hardcover version?

A lot of readers fuming over that question reminded me of their frustration in the aftermath of the latest flare-up between Amazon and the publishing industry. On Wednesday [February 22, 2012], more than 4,000 e-titles sold by Independent Publishers Group [IPG], one of the nation's biggest independent book distributors, got pulled by Amazon as the result of a dispute over pricing. IPG's Kindle contract was up for renewal and Amazon sought to extract more favorable margins. IPG refused to cave and so, the impasse.

The Apple Deal

This constitutes the newest chapter in an old struggle over e-book pricing. For years, publishers had left the discounting decisions in the hands of retailers. Then Steve Jobs came knocking. Apple's CEO [chief executive officer] wanted to make sure that iPad owners would have an alternative to buying e-books through Amazon and in 2010 he offered an intriguing idea that he said would benefit the book publishing industry.

While they wait for trustbusters on both sides of the Atlantic to finish their investigations, book publishers are desperate to hold the line [on e-book prices].

The specter of an increasingly powerful Amazon already loomed on the horizon. And while the publishers wanted to sell new hardcover titles at higher prices, Amazon, keen to sell more Kindles, was heavily discounting e-book titles, sometimes even at a loss. Explaining why the publishers would do better to change their business model, Jobs, as always, was the beneficiary of superb timing. From [author] Walter Isaacson's authorized biography:

> We told the publishers "We'll go to the agency model, where you set the price, and we get our 30 percent, and yes, the customer pays a little more, but that's what you want anyway," Isaacson quotes Jobs as saying. "But we also asked for a guarantee that if anybody else is selling the books cheaper than we are, then we can sell them at the lower price too. So they went to Amazon and said, 'You're going to sign an agency contract or we're not going to give you the books.'"

The pitch worked. Henceforth, book publishers, not the retailers, would call the shots. Was this in the best interests of consumers? The Justice Department [DOJ] is asking that very same question. While the EU [European Union] presses a separate investigation the DOJ has opened a probe. A representative for the department declined comment other than to confirm that the "investigation is ongoing."

While they wait for trustbusters on both sides of the Atlantic to finish their investigations, book publishers are desperate to hold the line. But they also face another challenge to their newly imposed discount regime: It's only a matter of time before Amazon fully outgrows its origins as a middle-man.

It's already part of the way there. The company wants to become a full-fledged book publisher. It's opened publishing offices on both coasts and has signed a clutch of exclusive deals with best-selling author Timothy Ferriss and e-book publisher RosettaBooks. It also recently acquired 450 children's titles—probably not the last such deal it pursues.

Book Lovers for Amazon

No such ambiguity about assigning blame on the part of Kindle customers. They've already figured this one out.

"I buy many books each month from Amazon for my Kindle Fire," a reader named John Spellman wrote me. "The price of some books is ridiculous. $14.99 for a download when the same book, hardcover, is available from Book of the Month Club for $9.95. I stopped buying hardcover because I have no space to store books. The rip-off by publishers is sickening. I personally feel that no e-book should be more than $10. I am pleased that Amazon is challenging the price gougers."

It's a common refrain sounded by readers noting that while the marginal cost for selling an extra digital download is near zero, book publishers frequently price the digital versions only a few dollars below the hard-cover price.

"There is absolutely no reason for higher pricing on digital books," a reader posted in one of the CNET News talkback forums. "It's not like the author with a traditional publishing contract is making more money on digital media, even though they should be. This is simply about the publishing industry trying to make huge profits on digital copies that they have very little overhead for. It's no wonder so many authors are self-publishing their digital books and raking in 70 percent of the sales to boot. That's waaaay more money than they'd ever get from a traditional publishing contract. Even better, the author gets to control the rights to their own catalog of titles when they self-publish."

The amen corner will nod its assent, but the question remains: how much is a fair price to pay for an e-book? The boilerplate answer—whatever the market will bear—will not suffice. You can forget about the textbook definitions because this issue is going nuclear. A *lot* of people believe that charging $10 or more for the portability and convenience of an e-book is ridiculous. The book publishers haven't helped their cause by doing a poor job explaining their case. If they're not careful, they risk getting Napsterized [giving away another's products for free]. Though piracy has already started, it hasn't become rife. At least not yet.

If it comes down to Amazon and the DOJ on one side against Apple and the book publishers on the other, guess which side the book lovers will be rooting for?

Public Libraries Should Root for Amazon to Win the E-book Pricing War

PublicLibraries.com

PublicLibraries.com is a website that promotes the use and support of local public libraries in the United States.

Amazon and one of the largest independent book publishers, IPG [Independent Publishers Group], are currently battling to the death over ebook pricing. In a nutshell, Amazon wants ebook prices to be much lower. IPG wants ebook prices to be just a little less than print books.

Both parties seem unwilling to budge. Last week [February 22, 2012] negotiations came to a halt and Amazon stopped selling all 4,414 ebooks published by IPG over the pricing dispute.

The Amazon/IPG Dispute

The CEO [chief executive officer] of IPG, Curt Matthews, decided to draft a response titled "What Should an E-book Cost?" Matthews provided specific details on IPG's royalty, cost, and pricing structure for both print books and ebooks. This was his genuine effort to try to justify why ebooks should cost only a little less than print books. . . .

Amazon wants IPG to cease to exist. They want authors to self-publish their ebooks at Amazon instead.

If an author self-publishes and prices their ebook at $2.99 at Amazon, they will earn $2.09 (70 percent). To earn that same $2.09 going through a publisher, the author would have to price their ebook at $13.93!

That is so utterly inconceivable. The publishers want to charge 365 percent more than Amazon wants to charge. The author will get the same amount of money but the publisher will end up earning 50–70 percent of the total price. It's ironic that you can spell PIG with the name of the publisher that's fighting to take home the vast majority of the profit from the sale of an ebook. How can a publisher take home $7–$10 and pay the author $2 when Amazon is willing to take home $1 and pay the author $2? It's amazing that anyone would choose to go through a traditional book publisher anymore.

Matthews claims that a lot [of] that money goes to "the cost of editing, designing, page makeup, and proofreading" as well as the "office, and the warehouse, and the staff". These services do cost money, but authors choosing to self-publish can now hire independent editors and book creation services at very low cost. The services offered are often superior to those provided by the traditional book publishers too. When was the last time you read a book without a bunch of grammar and spelling errors?

Matthews points out that the larger publishers earn 70 percent on their ebook deals and that his firm is small and only makes 50 percent. He then states "Now Amazon is insisting on terms for both print books and e-books that are even less favorable for independent presses. How will such presses be able to afford to publish good books when they receive so little of the sales price? They won't be able to."

And that's exactly the idea. Amazon wants to put the book publishers out of business. Ebooks will cost about 79 percent less if they are successful. This is why public libraries and pretty much everyone else should be rooting for Amazon to win the ebook price war against the book publishers.

Publishers Must Price E-books Higher than Amazon to Cover Publishing Costs

Curt Matthews

Curt Matthews is the chief executive officer of the Independent Publishers Group, a large independent book and e-book publisher.

The conversation about the pricing and marketing of print books and e-books has not been well informed. Here is information about how the numbers actually run. The place to start is with print books.

What Should a Printed Book Cost?

The royalty rate is usually 10% of the cover price for a hardbound book, 7.5% for a paperback, increasing by a few percents if certain levels of sales are achieved. So an author makes $1.12 a copy on a $14.95 paperback. A 10,000 copy sale of that paperback—a very respectable performance in the estimation of most publishers—will earn the author about $11,000; not bad, except it takes a year or two of very hard work to write a book. Most authors have to keep their day jobs.

What does the publisher make? He will sell that $14.95 paperback to the booksellers and book wholesalers at, on average, a 50% discount from the price on the cover—$7.48 in the case of this $14.95 book. For 10,000 copies sold this will amount to $74,800. The printing of the 10,000 copies will run about $1.50 a copy or $15,000 total. We have calculated that the royalty for the author will be $11,000. So the publisher nets $48,000, not a bad day at the office except this income also has to cover the cost of that office, and the warehouse, and the staff. When all these factors are taken into account, the publisher's share is about the same as the author's.

A carefully kept secret in the book business is that even the best authors need editing. In fact the good ones insist on help and will follow a gifted editor from company to company to get it. Most books are hugely improved by the editorial process. Nor are the improvements editors make limited to spelling, punctuation, and grammar. Often they are deep structural changes that make a title more engaging for its intended audience, more saleable.

[E-books need] editorial services . . . [and must] be marketed, distributed, and publicized, just as a print edition must be.

The help that authors get is never mentioned in public because the author is the brand name, not the publisher. Spreading the credit among any more names would just blur the marketing focus. But the cost of editing, designing, page makeup, and proofreading is high, higher in fact than the cost of printing the book.

What Should an E-Book Cost?

What then should you pay for an e-book edition of a $14.95 paperback? Most people would say it ought to be practically nothing because there are no design, no printing, no warehousing, no shipping costs for the publisher to pay. An e-book, after all, is just a batch of electrons, weightless, shippable through a wire.

But this is to misunderstand what it takes to make a successful book. An e-book still needs all of the expensive editorial services noted above; and if it is going to sell, it has to be marketed, distributed, and publicized, just as a print edition must be. And the author royalty on an e-book sale is usually about the same as it is for a print book, even though the list price of the e edition is lower. We have noted that for our $14.95 paperback the printing amounts to about $1.50. Warehousing and shipping will add another $1.50 to the real cost of selling a printed book. A web retailer should be able to work on a narrower margin than a bricks and mortar bookstore, which could lower the price of an e-edition perhaps another $2.00.

Deduct these specifically print related costs from the price of a printed book and the minimum price for a straightforward e-book comes to about $10.00—less than the price of the print version but not some small fraction of the print price. Certainly not 99 cents, and not $5.00 either. E-books, as they become more important in the book trade, will have to carry their full share of the editorial and marketing costs of producing them.

Amazon's Terms

At the moment there are two very different ways publishers can work with Amazon: the Agency Model and the Wholesale Model. There has been a lot of fancy dancing around these models, but of course it all boils down to how the money is divided up between the parties. Only the six biggest publishing companies have had the market power to compel Amazon to accept the Agency Model, which allows the publisher to keep 70% of the e-book list price. Independent publishers have had to accept the Wholesale Model, which has let us keep only about 50% of the suggested price. That is a 20% difference.

Now Amazon is insisting on terms for both print books and e-books that are even less favorable for independent presses. How will such presses be able to afford to publish good books when they receive so little of the sales price? They won't be able to. And is it obvious that independent presses should have to work at such a huge competitive disadvantage to the major publishing houses?

Independent publishers are crucial to the vitality of our culture. They are the reason why in America almost no good author goes unpublished.

E-book Publishers May Lose by Keeping E-book Prices Artificially High

Mathew Ingram

Mathew Ingram is a journalist, columnist, blogger, and senior writer for GigaOM, a provider of online media, events, and research for global technology companies. He writes about business, technology, and all forms of media.

When the major book publishing firms signed an agreement with Apple that allowed them to control the prices for their e-books—unlike the deal they had with Amazon, which gave the online retailer the right to cut prices if it wanted to—they probably thought they had won a major battle. But as a *Wall Street Journal* [WSJ] story points out, they are still shooting themselves in the foot when it comes to e-book prices, by keeping them artificially high in an attempt to shore up their profit margins and protect their existing print business. In the long run, that pricing model could wind up doing far more damage than the model it replaced.

The *Journal* piece notes that e-book prices, particularly for some best-selling and popular titles, are in many cases actually higher than prices for the comparable print version. For example, author Ken Follett's *Fall of Giants* costs $18.99 as an e-book and sells on Amazon as a paperback for $16.50. One New Yorker says he is buying fewer e-books because of the higher prices publishers are charging for them, telling the *Journal*:

> It's hard to justify the purchase of e-books that are priced at $10 to $15 when you can buy the real book on Amazon used for $2 or $3

Publishers Are Indulging
in Wishful Thinking

And how do publishers justify doing this? Among other things, they claim that consumers are actually willing to pay more for the e-book version of a novel because of the convenience and other features that they get with an electronic edition—the ability to search, make highlights, and so on. A senior vice-president at Hachette Digital, a unit of one of the world's largest publishing firms, tells the *Journal* that she believes "there has been a change in the understanding of the value of a digital book," and that readers see the added value and are willing to pay extra for it.

Sales in some cases can jump by as much as 20 times when the price drops.

This sounds like a giant case of wishful thinking, and there is mounting evidence to indicate it is just that. While it's true that e-book sales continue to increase, that's more likely due to the mainstream adoption of readers like the Kindle and the iPad than it is any acceptance of higher e-book prices. The *WSJ* piece also quotes publishing industry sources as saying they are seeing consumer resistance to e-book prices in the $10 to $15 range, and a company that tracks e-book piracy notes that the rate with which books are being scanned and uploaded to file-sharing sites is also increasing exponentially.

But another publishing industry insider has a warning that is even more important for traditional publishers than piracy: Lorraine Shanley says that high prices for mainstream e-books could easily convince more readers to try self-published novels from authors using Amazon's Kindle publishing platform—since many of them are priced at $5 or cheaper. Self-publishing success stories such as Amanda Hocking and John Locke have shown that sales in some cases can jump by as much as 20 times when the price drops.

Does Amazon Need Another Stick to Beat Publishers With?

That's the real threat for publishers with their antiquated pricing models: Amazon is already eating into their market share on a number of fronts—by making the self-publishing of books as easy as possible (and offering self-publishers monetary incentives to sign deals with Amazon) and by signing up authors to its own digital imprints. Do publishers really want to give the company even more power by pushing consumers of their books away with artificially high prices? Do they need to give Amazon another stick to beat them with?

The irony in this approach, as the *WSJ* story points out, is that the "agency model" that the major publishers signed with Apple actually results in *less* money from many titles. In the past, Amazon would give publishers a fixed price for both the printed and the electronic version of a book, and then any discounting on the e-book version would come out of Amazon's pocket. But under the agency model, publishers get 70 percent of the retail price, which for some titles means they wind up with less revenue.

On top of that, the Big Six publishing firms are currently embroiled in a federal antitrust investigation over the agency model, based on allegations that the deal with Apple represented collusion and illegal price-fixing and is therefore anticompetitive. Winning the ability to set prices for e-books instead of letting Amazon do so may have felt like a victory at the time, but it could turn out to be a hollow one.

Amazon's Predatory Pricing Could Destroy Bookstores and Print Book Publishers

Husna Haq

Husna Haq is a correspondent for the Christian Science Monitor, *which covers global news in a weekly news magazine and on the organization's website, csmonitor.com.*

M ight Apple's agency model—in the crosshairs of a [US] Justice Department investigation over price fixing— actually encourage competition rather than kill it?

That's the latest question circulating publishing forums and tech blogs since last Thursday's [March 8, 2012] news that the Justice Department may be close to filing an antitrust lawsuit against Apple and five publishers. What's more, interested parties like the Authors Guild, a writers' advocate group, are coming forward to defend Apple's agency model.

"The irony bites hard," writes Authors Guild President Scott Turow in an open letter defending the agency model. "Our government may be on the verge of killing real competition in order to save the appearance of competition."

Agency vs. Wholesale Pricing

Let's back up. The DOJ [US Department of Justice] is threatening to file a lawsuit against five publishers (Hachette Book Group, Simon & Schuster, Macmillan, Penguin, and Harper Collins) and one distributer (Apple), all operating under the agency model and all suspected of e-book price collusion.

There are two competing models for distributing books, print or electronic: the wholesale model and the agency model.

Under the wholesale model, a publisher sells its goods to a distributor for a fixed price and the distributor is free to decide the actual price for the public (including selling at negative margins to dump books on the marketplace in the case of Amazon). Under the agency model, publishers set the retail price and the distributor gets a fee (30 percent in the case of Apple).

The problem, writes Turow of the Authors Guild, is that wholesale pricing gives distributors control at the expense of the publishing industry. "Amazon was using e-book discounting to destroy bookselling, making it uneconomic for physical bookstores to keep their doors open," he writes.

That's because the primary purpose of the wholesale model is to serve the retailer's (in this case, Amazon) interests, even if it means throwing publishers under the proverbial bus. (For example, it is in Amazon's interest to price-dump top-selling e-books at a loss in order to promote sales of other products or up-sell high-margin items through its recommendation engine, writes *Guardian* tech reporter Frederic Filloux.) What's more, the wholesale model is deflationary, encouraging retailers to push margins ever lower to attract and capture customers. That threatens physical books, and with it, bricks-and-mortar bookstores, writes Turow of the Authors Guild.

Amazon was using e-book discounting to destroy bookselling, making it uneconomic for physical bookstores to keep their doors open.

He explains Amazon's pricing scheme in detail:

"Just before Amazon introduced the Kindle, it convinced major publishers to break old practices and release books in digital form at the same time they released them as hardcovers. Then Amazon dropped its bombshell: as it announced the launch of the Kindle, publishers learned that Amazon would be selling countless frontlist e-books at a loss. This was a game-changer, and not in a good way. Amazon's predatory pricing would shield it from e-book competitors that lacked Amazon's deep pockets. Critically, it also undermined the hardcover market that brick-and-mortar stores depend on. It was as if Netflix announced that it would stream new movies the same weekend they opened in theaters. Publishers, though reportedly furious, largely acquiesced. Amazon, after all, already controlled some 75% of the online physical book market."

It's no wonder, he writes, that when Apple entered the market with its iPad and Apple's newly-pioneered Agency plan, publishers "leapt at Apple's offer and clung to it like a life raft. . . . [I]t was seize the agency model or watch Amazon's discounting destroy their physical distribution chain."

It's unclear whether or not the publishing industry colluded in entering the agency model, but it appears it did move in accordance with its best interests. And, if we are to believe Turow's argument, with the best interests of readers and bricks-and-mortar bookstores.

Whether the DOJ reconsiders its lawsuit or continues to pursue Apple and its agency model remains to be seen.

The US Department of Justice E-book Lawsuit Will Have Little Effect on Price Competition

Matthew Yglesias

Matthew Yglesias is a business and economics correspondent for Slate, *an online magazine of news, politics, and culture.*

This week [April 11, 2012], the United States Justice Department filed a lawsuit against Apple and several book publishers, alleging they had colluded to raise e-book prices after launching the iPad. A few publishers settled out of court, but Apple and the publishing houses Penguin and Macmillan will reportedly fight to protect the right of publishers, rather than vendors like Amazon, to set e-book prices. Last month, [commentator] Matthew Yglesias argued that even if Apple did fix prices with publishers, it's unlikely to have much of an effect on competition in the book business. The full piece is reprinted below:

A bit buried in [the recent] iPad 3 excitement was the news that Apple, along with five major American book publishers, was given notice by the Justice Department that it's about to be sued for colluding to raise prices. A tech giant can afford to shrug off something as petty as an anti-trust lawsuit over books, but for HarperCollins, Penguin, Macmillan, Hachette, and Simon & Schuster (full disclosure: my publisher) the implications are potentially quite dire. Scott Turow, president of the Authors Guild, went further and argued that "everyone who cherishes a rich literary culture" should be alarmed by the DOJ's actions. He's wrong. If there's a case against the government's actions it's that the forces of disruption buffeting traditional publishing are much too large to be blocked by any cartel. The good news is that literary culture should survive either way.

A for-profit company like industry leader Amazon doesn't want to give tons of books away for free.

Pricing Digital Books

The basic question here is, how much should a digital book cost? A traditional book is, among other things, a rather heavy manufactured product. Like many manufactured goods, it's much more efficient to make a whole bunch of books at once rather than crafting them one at a time on demand. Consequently, to bring a book to market a traditional publisher needs to make a substantial up-front investment in inventory, and that inventory then needs to be lugged around the country. If consumer demand turns out to be low (the sad fate of my first book), then unsold copies end up languishing in warehouses. Factor in the retailers' rent and labor costs plus their desire for a profitable markup, and it's clear that each copy needs to be fairly expensive or the whole business will collapse.

Digital books are not like that. There are fixed costs associated with getting the book together in the first place, but selling five copies costs about the same as selling 5,000 or 5 million. A properly motivated individual or organization might even give a digital book away for free the way the Center for Economic and Policy Research's Dean Baker did last year.

A for-profit company like industry leader Amazon doesn't want to give tons of books away for free, but they do have interests beyond pricing things at a profit-maximizing level.

They'd like people to buy Kindles, for example, and they want as many folks as possible to start reading digital books. That's why they launched the Kindle with a mandate that books be sold for a flat rate of $9.99 even when charging more in specific cases might have made more sense. And that's also why they ignore bandwidth and storage costs and give public domain books away for free.

Publishers were, of course, free not to release Kindle editions of their titles, but most could see the need to get on the digital bandwagon. This was a very dangerous situation for major publishers. They'd gone from lording it over a landscape of thousands of independent retailers to dealing with just a handful of major chains. Now they were threatened with being suppliers to a monopsony purchaser of e-books, perennially stuck under Amazon's thumb. Enter Apple, the tech giant with an insatiable appetite to "control the whole widget." Even though the Kindle Reader for iPad is, in my opinion, the very best way in the whole world to read books, Apple wanted its own iBooks store. And to get it, they were prepared to give publishers what they wanted—the right to set their own prices, in exchange for sending a hefty 30 percent cut to Cupertino, Calif.

No Threat to Competition

So far, so good. Except the government is alleging that Apple didn't just show up offering a better deal. They're saying it actively colluded with the five major publishers to raise prices.

Turow and the Authors Guild say they have no idea whether collusion happened. Either way, they argue, the higher prices are good because they're helping to keep physical booksellers in business. "In bookstores," Turow writes, "readers are open to trying new genres and new authors: It's by far the best way for new works to be discovered."

I share my colleague Farhad Manjoo's skepticism that old-fashioned bookstores are all that great. Turow should also consider the fact that e-books can be advantageous for new authors. In the digital realm, an author can make a short piece available for little or no money as a loss-leader for potential future works. And digital sellers have no shortage of "shelf space" that has to be dedicated to a handful of specially favored books. The back catalog can live forever, and sales can come from the long tail of niche tastes.

What makes a major publishing house a major publishing house is its expertise in the manufacture and distribution of books.

Conversely, whatever the facts of the case, the Justice Department's notion that we should fear a book publishers' cartel is borderline absurd, on par with worrying about price-fixing in the horse-and-buggy market.

What makes a major publishing house a major publishing house is its expertise in the manufacture and distribution of books. As an ancillary element of the business, publishers are also good at recruiting authors, editing prose, and publicizing new works. But firms with expertise in writing, editing, and publishing text are a dime a dozen. [The online magazine] *Slate* has that know-how, as does every newspaper and magazine in the country and a huge quantity of independent and university presses. Even more troubling for traditional publishers, famous authors now have unprecedented ability to simply bypass the entire publishing system. If Suzanne Collins wants to sell a *Hunger Games* prequel directly to her readers, does anyone doubt she'd sell vast quantities? Celebrities could even potentially become their own publishing brands, using their fame to substitute for a traditional market apparatus. Oprah Winfrey has a proven ability to drive book sales. Why not launch an Oprah Press?

That's not to say the six big publishers are doomed to go extinct. But the only way for these firms to stay viable is to publish books people like and to sell them at a price readers want to pay. Whether they merge, collude, or simply find a convenient confluence of interests around Apple's efforts to compete with Amazon, there's no real threat to competition here. Literary culture, for better or for worse, is dealing with a radically transformed business landscape. The Justice Department is, at best, irrelevant to this process.

CHAPTER 4

What Is the Future for E-books?

Chapter Preface

Part of the major transformation in the publishing world by e-books is the dramatic increase in the number of self-published books. In the past, authors who were rejected by book publishers rarely considered self-publishing because without the validation and marketing exposure provided by an established publishing company, sales would likely be limited. Today, however, e-books and Amazon's self-publishing program allow authors to self-publish and offer their writings to people around the world via Amazon's online, global bookstore. One person who has taken advantage of this new self-publishing opportunity is Amanda Hocking, an American author who wrote vampire novels and became an international phenomenon by selling her books on Amazon. As of early 2012, Hocking had sold over one and a half million books and earned $2.5 million from her self-published works.

Born in 1984, Hocking grew up in rural Minnesota, reading books from the local library or from rummage sales. By her teens, she had begun writing her own books and sending them to publishers. Despite receiving many rejection letters, Hocking continued to write, amassing seventeen unpublished novels. In 2009, she committed to writing every night while working a day job caring for disabled people. Finally, in 2010, desperately wanting to go to Chicago to see an exhibition about Jim Henson, creator of the Muppets, Hocking decided to put her books on Amazon, hoping to raise a few hundred dollars to go to the exhibition. She helped to market her books by writing a blog and posting on Twitter and Facebook, and she also made her books available to the Barnes & Noble Nook, Sony E-reader, and Apple iBook markets. Within six months of listing on Amazon, Hocking had made enough money to go to Chicago and an additional $20,000 by selling a hundred-fifty thousand copies of her books. Her books continued to sell thereafter, making her a multimillionaire in less than two years.

Hocking's financial success can be attributed partly to her decision to adopt a pricing policy in which she charged only $0.99 for the first book in a series, in order to attract readers. Sequels, however, she priced at $2.99. Although these prices might seem incredibly low compared to the prices of printed books, Amazon's self-publishing policies pay authors more of the profits than traditional publishers. Amazon paid Hocking 30 percent in royalties for her $0.99 books, but 70 percent in royalties for the $2.99 sequels.

Hocking became an icon in the new digital publishing world; however, other writers have similarly profited significantly from the e-book self-publishing medium. These include H.P. Mallory, also an American paranormal novelist; German novelist Oliver Potzsch, who benefited from an Amazon program that publishes translations of foreign novels; and novelist J.A. Konrath, who also writes a blog for new authors. In fact, a recent survey found that nineteen of the twenty-five bestselling e-book authors on Amazon had never been published by traditional publishers. Some commentators see this trend as a bad sign for traditional publishing companies, which historically provided the only path to success for aspiring writers. However, after publishing numerous times on Amazon, Amanda Hocking in 2011 signed a four-book deal with a traditional publisher, St. Martin's Press, reportedly worth at least $2 million. The Amazon program for self-publishing e-books, some observers suggest, could end up providing just another route into the traditional publishing world. The future, therefore, might be good for both self-publishing and traditional publishing companies. The authors of the viewpoints included in this chapter discuss the e-book self-publishing revolution and other current and potential future impacts of e-books.

The Future of Writing Is Digital

Sam Harris

Sam Harris is the author of several New York Times *bestselling books and a cofounder and chief executive officer of Project Reason, a nonprofit foundation dedicated to spreading scientific knowledge and secular values.*

Writers, artists, and public intellectuals are nearing some sort of precipice: Their audiences increasingly expect digital content to be free. [Author] Jaron Lanier has written and spoken about this issue with great sagacity. You can purchase his book, which most of you will not do, or you can watch him discuss these matters for free. The problem is thus revealed even in the act of stating it. How can a person like Lanier get paid for being brilliant? This has become an increasingly difficult question to answer.

A Digital Future

Where publishing is concerned, the Internet is both midwife and executioner. It has never been easier to reach large numbers of readers, but these readers have never felt more entitled to be informed and entertained for free. I have been very slow to appreciate these developments, and yet it is clear even to me that there are reasons to fear for the life of the printed book. Needless to say, many of the changes occurring in publishing are changes that neither publishers nor authors want. The market for books is continually shifting beneath our feet, and nobody knows what the business of publishing will look like a decade from now.

When I published *The End of Faith* in 2004, I created a website as an afterthought. In fact, I remember feeling silly asking my publisher to put the web address on the dust jacket, not knowing if there was any point in doing so. While my website has since become the hub of everything I have accomplished as an author, it took me years to understand its utility, and I only began blogging a few months ago. Clearly, I am a slow learner. But many other authors are still pretending that the Internet doesn't exist. Some will surely see their careers suffer as a result. One fact now seems undeniable: The future of the written word is (mostly or entirely) digital.

The truth is, I now expect [print magazine] content to be free.

The Decline of Print Journalism

Journalism was the first casualty of this transformation. How can newspapers and magazines continue to make a profit? Online ads don't generate enough revenue and paywalls are intolerable; thus, the business of journalism is in shambles. Even though I sympathize with the plight of publishers—and share it by association as a writer—as a reader, I am without pity. If your content is behind a paywall, I will get my news elsewhere. I subscribe to the print edition of *The New Yorker*, but when I want to read one of its articles online, I find it galling to have to login and wrestle with its proprietary e-reader. The result is that I read and reference *New Yorker* articles far less frequently than I otherwise would. I've been a subscriber for 25 years, but *The New Yorker* is about to lose me. What can they do? I don't know. The truth is, I now expect their content to be free.

My friend Christopher Hitchens is a writer of truly incandescent prose whose career has been forged almost entirely in the context of print journalism. Among his many outlets, the most prominent has probably been *Vanity Fair*: a gorgeous, glossy magazine to which I also subscribe. Happily, *Vanity Fair* offers its content for free on its website. I visited the site a moment ago and read Hitch's latest: a very tender essay of praise for the work of Joan Didion—another wonderful writer who, I have just learned from Hitch, will soon publish a book about the tragic death of her daughter. This will be a follow up to *The Year of Magical Thinking*, her searing account of the loss of her husband. I will buy and read Didion's new book, just as I bought and read the last one, and I expect that it will be a bestseller. Hitch did his job and got paid. Didion will soon publish her book in hardcover and has already benefited from his review. All appears to be well in the Kingdom of Print.

[Social media is] the death knell for traditional publishing.

However, with the gimlet eyes of a new blogger, I detect ominous portents of change. First, I see that Hitch's article has been featured on the *Vanity Fair* website for the better part of a week and has garnered only 813 Facebook likes and 75 Tweets. Many of my blog articles receive more engagement than this, some by nearly a factor of 10. No doubt this has something to do with the ratio of signal to noise: When readers come to a personal blog, they are more or less guaranteed to read what the author has written. How many people will find Hitch's article on the *Vanity Fair* website? Of course, it is prominently displayed on the home page, along with an arresting photo of Didion taken by Annie Leibovitz, one of the most famous photographers on earth. Presumably, Leibovitz had to go to Didion's apartment with a small crew to obtain this image. All of this creative work was paid for, one imagines, by print ads. But with respect to Hitch's interests as a writer, and Didion's as his subject, everything else in the current issue of *Vanity Fair* is noise. A glance at the online page rank of the magazine raises even greater concerns. I know bloggers—Tim Ferriss and Seth Godin, for instance—whose personal blogs get more traffic than the entire *Vanity Fair* website.

If your book is 600-pages-long, you are demanding more of my time than I feel free to give.

When I began writing the previous paragraph, I forwarded Hitch's article on Facebook and Twitter. Over 3000 people have since followed the link I sent, and we're up to 955 Facebook likes and 100 Tweets. I hesitate to read too much into these metrics, but it doesn't seem entirely crazy to wonder whether a significant percentage of the people who have read Hitch's essay in the last week read it in the last hour because I broadcast it on social media. I used to view this as a wonderful synergy—digital enables print; print points back to digital; and both thrive. I now consider it the death knell for traditional publishing.

In between working for free and working for my publisher, I've begun to experiment with self publishing short ebooks.

Vanity Fair has a print circulation of around 1 million copies; the current issue has a fresh photo of Angelina Jolie on its cover; and Hitch is one of the best writers to ever draw breath. However, I'm reasonably sure that this blog post, or the next one, will reach more readers than his latest gem. For bloggers like Ferriss and Godin, the future arrived long ago: Publishing in *Vanity Fair* would be tantamount to burying their work. This is astounding. Given its range of content, and the costs of acquiring this content, a magazine like *Vanity Fair* should get much more traffic than any one person's blog. And this brings us back to the problem of money: Apart from my occasional use of a webmaster and a graphic designer, my blog employs no one—not even me. Where is all this heading? I can count on one finger the number of places where it is still obviously better for me to publish than on my own blog— the opinion page of *The New York Times*. But it's not so much better that I've been tempted to send them an article in the last few months. Is this just the hubris of the blogosphere? Maybe—but not for everyone and not for long.

Difficulties for Physical Books

Related difficulties are now looming for books. I love physical books as much as anyone. And when I really want to get a book into my brain, I now purchase both the hardcover and electronic editions. From the point of view of the publishing industry, I am the perfect customer. This also makes me a very important canary in the coal mine—and I'm here to report that I've begun to feel woozy. For instance, I've started to think that most books are too long, and I now hesitate before buying the next big one. When shopping for books, I've suddenly become acutely sensitive to the opportunity costs of reading any one of them. If your book is 600-pages-long, you are demanding more of my time than I feel free to give. And if I could accomplish the same change in my view of the world by reading a 60-page version of your argument, why didn't you just publish a book this length instead?

The honest answer to this last question should disappoint everyone: Publishers can't charge enough money for 60-page books to survive; thus, writers can't make a living by writing them. But readers are beginning to feel that this shouldn't be their problem. Worse, many readers believe that they can just jump on YouTube and watch the author speak at a conference, or skim his blog, and they will have absorbed most of what he has to say on a given subject. In some cases this is true and suggests an enduring problem for the business of publishing. In other cases it clearly isn't true and suggests an enduring problem for our intellectual life.

These intersecting concerns have now led me to stratify my written work: I am currently writing a traditional, printed book for my mainstream publisher, the Free Press. At the other extreme, I do a lot of writing for free, almost entirely on my blog. In between working for free and working for my publisher, I've begun to experiment with self publishing short ebooks. Last week, I published *LYING*, my first installment in this genre. The results have been simultaneously thrilling and depressing.

My goal in *LYING* was to write a very accessible essay on an important topic that could be absorbed in one sitting. I know how revolutionary it is to be honest with everyone one meets—to refuse to shade the truth even slightly in business or in one's personal life—and I know how few people do this. *LYING* spells out my reasons for thinking that we would all be better off living this way.

The essay appears to have had its desired effect on many readers. But others were not satisfied. Some did not understand the format—a very short book that can be read in 40 minutes—and expected to get a much longer book for $1.99. Many wondered why it is available only as an ebook. Some fans of ebooks were powerfully aggrieved to find it available only on the Kindle platform—they own Nooks, or detest Amazon for one reason or another. However, the fact is that Amazon made it extraordinarily easy for me to do this; the Kindle Single is the perfect format for so short a book; and Kindle content can be read on every computer and almost any handheld device. I decided that it was not worth my time or other people's money to publish *LYING* elsewhere, or as a physical book.

On the surface, the launch of *LYING* has been a great success. It reached the #1 spot for Kindle Singles immediately and #9 for all Kindle content. It is amazing to finish writing, hit "upload," and watch one's work soar and settle, however briefly, above the vampire novels and diet books.

I would be lying, however, if I said that I wasn't stung by some of the early criticism. Some readers felt that a 9000-word essay was not worth $1.99, especially when they can read my 5000-word blog posts for free. It is true that I put a lot of work into many of my blog posts, but *LYING* took considerably longer to write than any of them. It is a deceptively simple book—and I made it simple for a reason. Some of my readers seem not to have appreciated this and prefer to follow me into my usual thickets of argument and detail. That's fine. But it is, nevertheless, painful to lose a competition with oneself, especially over a difference of $1.99.

One thing is certain: writers and public intellectuals must find a way to get paid for what they do—and the opportunities to do this are changing quickly. My current solution is to write longer books for a traditional press and publish short ebooks myself on Amazon. If anyone has any better ideas, please publish them somewhere—perhaps on a blog—and then send me a link. And I hope you get paid.

E-books and Paper Books Will Coexist

Jan Swafford

Jan Swafford is a composer and an author of books on music.

Bold Prediction. Why e-books will never replace real books—because we perceive print and electronic media differently. Because Marshall McLuhan was right about some things.

McLuhan's Ideas About Media

In case you don't recall one of the more influential thinkers of the late 20th century: McLuhan was an academic media theorist who ended up being called a "high priest of popular culture." He was big enough to be a standing joke on *Laugh-In* ("Marshall McLuhan, what are you doin'?") to appear in a cameo in [the movie] *Annie Hall*, to get interviewed in *Playboy*. One of the fundamental things McLuhan said was that new media change us and change the world. We see that principle in every kind of technology. When films started to talk, we started to talk in their phrases and cadences. When musical notation was invented, it took music into new dimensions of complexity and length. When computers started to link up on the Internet . . . You get the idea.

McLuhan declared that the two epochal cultural developments of the last millennium were, first, the invention of movable type in the 15th century, which proliferated data in print and finally took humanity out of its primeval tribal culture (a culture that had already been shaken, millennia earlier, by the invention of writing). Second, the epochal change of the last two centuries was the advent of electric media, starting with the telegraph. From that point on, data started to blanket the globe at close to the speed of light.

One of McLuhan's central concepts is still intensely relevant in the age of Internet and e-books: his dichotomy of hot and cool media.

Relatively few prophecies pan out, and plenty of McLuhan's haven't. His peaceful, neo-tribal "global village" hasn't worked so well. He predicted the end of politics, parties, and elections. Yeah, right. Still, he was the first to realize the transformation TV wrought on politics. From the pioneering Kennedy/Nixon debates to rampant political advertising and the 24-hour news cycle, TV has become the strongest force in political life. It's long been understood that a prime reason Kennedy beat Nixon for the presidency was that Kennedy looked better on TV. Now a politician's image outstrips his or her ideas—outstrips his or her politics. Which is just what McLuhan predicted: TV is about gut feeling, not reason.

One of McLuhan's central concepts is still intensely relevant in the age of Internet and e-books: his dichotomy of hot and cool media. "A hot medium," he said, "is one that extends one single sense in 'high definition.'" The less audiovisual information we have to fill in ourselves, the hotter the medium. Books and movies are "hot" because they supply a high level of information to the eye. Telephone and TV are "cool" because the telephone gives the ear "a meager amount of information," and a TV screen is less high-def than a movie. The video image, in contrast to film, is constantly being redrawn as we watch it. In the cool medium of TV, our eye and brain have to create the illusion of a complete picture; that process sucks us in, starting at the level of our synapses.

Obviously, high-definition television, which McLuhan foresaw and mused about, complicates the distinction between hot and cool media. But I'd argue that his dichotomy endures.

There is a difference in how we perceive things in print and on an electronic screen. Watching TV has an innately mesmerizing effect that goes beyond whatever happens to be on. TV is addictive, druglike, in a way that movies and print aren't. Recall McLuhan's most famous aphorism: "The medium is the message." To a large extent, we respond to any medium as medium, quite apart from the content. I add that language reflects that: We "go to the movies"; we "watch TV"; we "read a book." If you're a book reader, you care more about reading itself than about any particular book.

We perceive words on-screen differently than in print.

McLuhan didn't think content was unimportant, but he believed the delivering technology is what ultimately involves and evolves us. "The 'message' of any medium or technology is the change of scale or pace or pattern that it introduces into human affairs." TV changed the world, in ways good and bad. And a computer screen is essentially a TV. Have you noticed the blank absorption on the faces of people watching TV (except, of course, for sports and politics)? It's much the same as people watching a computer screen.

McLuhan saw the first glimmers of the Internet and seemed to sense what was coming. He spoke of "a mosaic world in which space and time are overcome by television, jets, and computers—a simultaneous, 'all-at-once' world in which everything resonates with everything else in a total electrical field." But he may never have imagined the phenomenon of millions of people staring at a screen, not looking at TV shows but reading words on their computers, as you're doing now. That further blurs his cool-hot dichotomy. But I say again: We perceive words on-screen differently than in print. In the process of writing and teaching writing, I engage in regular experiments testing this theory.

Writing and Technology

Here's how it works, with me and with most writers I know (because I've asked). I've used computers for more than 25 years. I draft prose on-screen, work it over until I can't find much wrong with it, then double-space it and print it out. At that point I discover what's really there, which is ordinarily hazy, bloated, and boring. It looked pretty good on-screen, but it's crap. My first drafts on paper, after what amount to several drafts on computer, look like a battlefield. . . .

I've taught college writing classes for a long time, and after computers came in, I began to see peculiar stuff on papers that I hadn't seen before: obvious missing commas and apostrophes, when I was sure most of those students knew better. It dawned on me that they were doing all their work on-screen, where it's hard to see punctuation. I began to lecture them about proofing on paper, although, at first, I didn't make much headway. They were unused to dealing with paper until the final draft, and they'd been taught never to make hand corrections on the printout. They edited on-screen and handed in the hard copy without a glance.

[E-books] will be the future of history, biography, scholarship.

Handwriting is OK! I proclaimed. I love to see hand corrections! Then I noticed glitches in student writing that also resulted from editing on-screen: glaring word and phrase redundancies, forgetting to delete revised phrases, strangely awkward passages. I commenced an ongoing sermon: You see differently and in some ways better on paper than on computer. Your best editing is on paper. Try it and see if I'm right. You'll get a better grade. The last got their attention. The students were puzzled and skeptical at first, but the ones who tried it often ended up agreeing with me.

Still, none of this is black and white. For years, after I got a computer I held onto my romantic attachment to writing first drafts by hand on long legal sheets. Then halfway through a book-for-hire I got in deadline trouble and for the sake of time had to start drafting on computer. I discovered, to my chagrin, that drafting first on computer tended to come out better than by hand. Computer drafts were cleaner and crisper. But, after that, I also discovered, paper rules. The final polish, the nuances, the pithy phrases, the tightening of clarity and logic—those mostly come from revising on paper.

The Potential of E-books

Mind, this is not a screed against e-media and their potential. Readers like the links in *Slate* articles, and so do I. My next book, on Beethoven, is planned on the one hand as a traditional text between covers with analytical endnotes and on the other as what I'm calling a "three-dimensional book." The text will be amplified by the endnotes and further amplified by a Web site, which adds more ideas and information, musical examples in sound and score, a blog, and what have you. In the e-book version, footnotes will become links, either to the Web site or to background content downloaded along with the text.

This kind of e-medium, I suspect, will be the future of history, biography, scholarship. Among other things, it makes possible a book on, say, music that is in theory available to everybody: The text for general readers, links providing instant musical illustrations for nonmusicians, other links adding technical and glossing material for scholars and musicians. The possibilities are dazzling to contemplate. They're cool in every sense of the word.

But e-book Beethoven will of course be a much different experience than the same guy between covers. Garrison Keillor has said, "On the Internet we're all hummingbirds." We flit from place to place, taking a sip here and a sip there. That's swell, but it isn't the way to read [Jane] Austen, [William But-ler] Yeats, and [James] Joyce. My book on an iPad or whatever will be richer in worthwhile ways, but it will be less absorbing and probably less emotionally compelling. (I'm making an-other prophecy of my own, that the iPad, a TV screen, will win out over the Kindle and its "e-ink," because the iPad and its clones will be far more flexible.)

So real books and e-books will coexist. That has happened time and again with other new technologies that were proph-esied to kill off old ones. Autos didn't wipe out horses. Movies didn't finish theater. TV didn't destroy movies. E-books won't destroy paper and ink. The Internet and e-books may set back print media for a while, and they may claim a larger audience in the end. But a lot of people who care about reading will want the feel, the smell, the warmth, the deeper intellectual, emotional, and spiritual involvement of print.

The über-message Marshall McLuhan proclaimed is an-other idea of his that stands the test of time. New media change us, not only our ideas and lifestyles but our very ner-vous systems. "The basic thing to remember about the electric media is that they inexorably transform every sense ratio and thus recondition and restructure all our values and institu-tions." That's overstated maybe, but there's something to it. We should not be blind to those kinds of changes. "Under-standing is half the battle," McLuhan said. To understand me-dia is to get a handle on them, to direct them in better ways, personally and publicly. When a new medium comes on the scene, we have to be aware and beware.

E-books Are Already Creating a Self-Publishing Revolution

Deirdre Donahue

Deirdre Donahue is a reporter for USA Today, *a daily newspaper.*

In 2009, Michael Prescott's dream died, or so he thought.

After graduating from college in 1980, Prescott had labored for almost three decades to become a best-selling novelist, writing more than 20 books under various names. He enjoyed critical praise and some successes.

But when 25 publishers passed on buying his thriller *Riptide*, Prescott thought the gig was up. Then, on a whim, he decided to self-publish it as an e-book.

Today, the soft-spoken Prescott, 51, is living his dream. He is one of 15 self-published authors whose e-books, often selling for just 99 cents, have cracked the top 150 on *USA TODAY*'s Best-Selling Books list this year [2011], threatening to change the face of publishing.

For Prescott and a handful of others, the numbers add up. Prescott says he has earned more than $300,000 before taxes this year by selling more than 800,000 copies of his self-published e-books.

Five of Prescott's thrillers have logged a total of 42 weeks on *USA TODAY*'s best-seller list.

"If someone in this year had told me I was going make a lot of money with e-books, I wouldn't have believed him," Prescott says. "I thought maybe a couple of hundred dollars."

E-books are changing the way authors and readers connect.

Today, authors such as Prescott can bypass traditional publishers. They can digitally format their own manuscript, set a price and sell it to readers through a variety of online retailers and devices. Amazon sells e-books via its Kindle device and on its Kindle app for smartphones and computers. Barnes & Noble sells e-books through its Nook electronic reader device and app. There is also the Sony eReader, Apple's iPad and Kobo, while Overdrive provides e-books to libraries.

Almost every day brings more digital modes for readers to obtain books in non-print forms, creating more choices for readers, opportunities for self-published writers, and challenges for traditional publishers.

[E-books are] ... creating more choices for readers, opportunities for self-published writers, and challenges for traditional publishers.

E-book Business Is Booming

According to the Association of American Publishers, e-books grew from 0.6% of the total trade market share in 2008 to 6.4% in 2010, the most recent figures available. Total net revenue for 2010: $878 million with 114 million e-books sold. In adult fiction, e-books are now 13.6% of the market.

"It's a gold rush out there," Prescott says. "Forty acres and a mule. It's the best time for an independent writer to get out there."

Forget the sensitive auteur waiting for the muse. Self-publishing an e-book requires an entrepreneurial spirit. For each 99-cent e-book sold, Prescott receives 35 cents. The online retailers—Amazon, BN.com, Apple, Sony—take the rest.

In traditional publishing, an unknown first-time author might get an advance of as little as $5,000, and then receive royalties from sales.

Prescott symbolizes how the Web can empower an author to circumvent the traditional business model, in which an author signs with an agent, who then sells the manuscript to a publisher, who edits, prints and distributes the book to stores and promotes it to the media in exchange for a share of the profits.

In the past, if the manuscript was rejected, it usually sat unread in a writer's desk drawer because the alternative—self-publishing one's book—carried a stigma. A writer would pay a vanity publisher to print the book, but stores rarely stocked them and critics rarely reviewed them.

Prescott was never willing to self-publish his print books. "From the start of my career, I was published by major publishing houses," he says. In 2000, Prescott's *The Shadow Hunter*—a thriller about a woman on the trail of a stalker—hit *USA TODAY*'s list at No. 140. His 1992 book *Shiver* was made into a 2011 movie.

But in the new world of "indie publishing," with its opportunity for self-published authors to sell hundreds of thousands of e-books, the stigma is disappearing. Plus, there are fewer fixed costs: no paper, no printing press, no warehouse, no trucks.

"It's a whole new world," Prescott says. "You're eliminating the middleman."

The balance of power [is] shift[ing] within publishing, with authors gaining more control over their work.

One reason Prescott is able to capitalize on the e-book revolution is that he already has a back list of novels previously edited and released by traditional publishers. (When his publisher let the book go out of print, the rights reverted to Prescott.)

"It's a Paradigm Shift"

Barbara Freethy, a top romance writer for 20 years who has written 30 novels, says that this year, she has sold 1.3 million self-published e-book versions of 17 of her out-of-print novels. Nine hit *USA TODAY*'s top 150.

"There have been more changes in the last two years than in the previous 18 years I have been in publishing," says the San Francisco writer, who is considering self-publishing her new book, *A Secret Wish*. She finds it satisfying to see the balance of power shift within publishing, with authors gaining more control over their work.

"It's a paradigm shift and a revolution," says J.A. Konrath, who is considered the guru of the self-publishing movement. "It's a huge win for readers," who now have easier access to more writers from around the world, he says.

Konrath, 41, who had modest success writing mysteries published by several traditional publishers (who still publish him), is now also a best-selling writer of self-published e-books. He also runs the influential website The Newbie's Guide to Publishing.

"I am a guy who had his butt kicked by the industry for 20 years, and now I'm showing other authors what they can do so they don't have to go through the same thing," he says. "Traditional book publishers are just serving drinks on the Titanic."

Konrath has seen his income from his self-published e-book sales go from $1,400 in April 2009 to $68,000 in April 2011.

But before you quit your day job to become a best-selling e-book writer, Konrath points out that the vast number of books released in any form, print or e-book, don't sell. To become a successful writer, talent, hard work and self-promotion are important. But publishing remains, at heart, a lottery. "I've always had that caveat. You have to get lucky," he says.

Meet attorney and debut novelist Darcie Chan, 37. This year, she self-published her debut novel, *The Mill River Recluse*, after being rejected by more than 100 literary agents. Set in a small Vermont town, the moody mystery centers on what happened to a beautiful young bride. It spent 16 weeks on *USA TODAY*'s best-seller list, peaking at No. 6. Chan says she has sold 416,000 copies of the 99-cent e-book.

Despite the success of some self-published e-book authors, it's premature to write the final chapter for traditional publishers. In an ironic twist, several self-published e-book superstars—most famously Amanda Hocking—have landed headline-making contracts with major publishing houses, which will be releasing their titles in print and digital formats.

Hocking, 27, a life-long Minnesotan from a working-class background, has been telling stories almost since she could climb out of the crib and was writing full-fledged novels at 17.

Unable to find an agent, she began self-publishing her young-adult paranormal romances in 2010. They became huge hits; seven of them have spent 50 weeks on *USA TODAY*'s list this year.

With technology enabling everyone to be his or her own Johannes Gutenberg, why would an author sign with a traditional book publisher?

Steppingstone to Success

Her addictive Trylle trilogy—*Switched, Torn* and *Ascend*, starring a raven-haired royal beauty named Wendy—has surged to the top with an intensity that suggests *Twilight*'s Bella has a rival for the hearts of female readers.

This is when things get weird. Already wealthy from her self-published e-books, Hocking in June signed a $2 million contract with St. Martin's Press. In January, the Trylle trilogy will hit stores—brick and mortar as well as online—in trade paperback. The movie rights already have been sold.

With technology enabling everyone to be his or her own Johannes Gutenberg, why would an author sign with a traditional book publisher?

"I wanted to reach more readers," Hocking says. She points out that most people—particularly the young teens she writes for—do not own iPads or e-readers. Hocking says it's about the story, not the device. "I wanted to write a fun book, not start a revolution."

C.J. Lyons also appreciates what traditional publishers bring to the table. A former emergency-room pediatrician, Lyons, 47, has published more than a dozen medical suspense novels with traditional publishers, as well as nine self-published titles, two of which hit *USA TODAY*'s list this summer.

Now she has signed with a traditional publisher, Minotaur Press, a division of St. Martin's. "I enjoy working with an editor, and I think my writing is ready to go to the next level," she says.

Her new publisher, Andrew Martin, says, "I'm not buying a book, I'm building a career with an author." He says an established publishing house lets the author do what he does best—write—while the publisher offers expert marketing, editing, production and aggressive protection against e-books being illegally pirated.

In the midst of this revolution, Martin sees a silver lining for traditional publishers. In the past, editors, agents and publishers depended on their gut about whether a book would connect with readers. Now the stories are being pre-tested in the online marketplace. "It's like the old-fashioned slush pile being road tested—with the cream rising to top."

In the end, Martin selected Lyons for the oldest reason of all.

"She is a storyteller. I think that speaks most to me."

Five E-book Trends That Will Change the Future of Publishing

Philip Ruppel

Philip Ruppel is president of McGraw-Hill Professional, a global publisher of print and electronic content and services for the business, scientific, technical, and medical communities.

Without a doubt, the e-book is practically the biggest thing that's hit the publishing industry since the invention of movable type. Publishers and e-book resellers are reporting astronomical growth.

At McGraw-Hill, we have been an active player in e-book technology dating back to devices like the RocketBook (one of the first e-book readers) that was launched more than 10 years ago. And today, e-books and e-book distribution is central to our publishing and growth strategy.

From the front lines of the e-book revolution, here are five trends I'm watching.

1. Enhanced E-Books Are Coming and Will Only Get Better. Consumers have already shown that they love e-books for their convenience and accessibility, but ultimately most e-books today are the same as print, just in digital form. The e-book of the not-too-distant future will be much more than text. Interactivity has arrived and will change the nature of the e-book.

Imagine video that shows how to fix a leaky faucet or solve complex math problems in statistics; audio that pronounces foreign language words as you read them, and assessment that lets you check what you remember and comprehend what you just read. These interactive features and more are being developed now and will be on the market in a matter of weeks, not months.

Consumers will care less about the device and more about the user experience of the e-reader.

Publishers are already conjuring up designs for the enhanced e-book of the future. Imagine still: If you miss five questions on your geometry test, will your book adapt and change to help you learn the questions and concepts you missed? Will your new novel provide a platform for live exchange with reading groups where you can discuss the book with the author? Today's enhanced e-books that feature talking heads or out-takes from movies are yesterday's ideas. Consumers will expect a much greater experience.

2. The Device War Is Nearly Over. Devices are proliferating to the point of confusion. Does a consumer buy a Nook, Kindle, Sony e-reader, an iLex or any one of 20 other dedicated e-readers? Or do they buy an iPad, Galaxy Tab, or other Android tablet? Or do they buy an e-reader at all? Have you ever noticed on a crowded train or bus how many people are reading their phone? And for a growing number of readers, the mobile phone is fine for reading just about anything. But as far as devices go, consumer confusion is likely to drive quick consolidation around a few winners in the market—no one wants to own the next "Betamax for books."

Because most developers are developing e-reader software that will work on multiple other devices (Kindle also works on the iPad, iPhone, and computers, for example), consumers will care less about the device and more about the user experience of the e-reader software, portability of titles from one device to another, and access to a full catalog of titles.

3. The $9.99 E-Book Won't Last Forever. Amazon popularized the $9.99 price point for best-seller trade titles, driving the widespread consumer adoption of the Kindle and con- sumption of e-books. This has caused confusion among many consumers who simply think every e-book should be $9.99 or less. But the majority of titles offered on Amazon are priced above $9.99, especially those with unique interactive features. For professional and technical publishers like McGraw-Hill, our e-books cannot stand the low, mass market pricing some consumers think should be applied to every e-book. Our costs are invested in extensive product and editorial development of sophisticated and technical content; the cost of paper, print- ing, and binding are a fraction of the real expense. And for some very specific and technical subject areas, our markets are much smaller. We simply couldn't afford to publish the work if it must be priced at the everyday low, low price of $9.99.

The real opportunity for publishers will be to develop e-books that offer the kind of interactive features mentioned above. Our customers will demand interactive books that pro- vide a much better, more informed and enriching experience. For them, the experience (not the cost) is often the primary driver.

4. The Contextual Upsell Will be a Business Model to Watch. E-books allow publishers to interact with their customers in new ways. Imagine customers who are trying to learn statistics and get stuck on a particular formula. They ask friends but no one can explain it well. They're stuck.

They click a help button, which points them to the pub- lisher site where they can download relevant tutorials about specific formulas for $2.99. They choose the one they need and get a new learning tool, which helps them progress in their class. Multiply this by hundreds of thousands of students who share similar learning gaps who will purchase through the book ("in-book app purchase") and it becomes an inter- esting new marketing opportunity.

5. Publishers Will Be More Important Than Ever. Despite the hype around self-publishing via the web, publishing houses will play an even greater role in an e-book world. Commodity content is everywhere (and largely free), so high-quality vetted, edited content—which takes a staff of experts—will be worth a premium.

At McGraw-Hill, the average technical and reference book engages teams of editors, copy editors, proofreaders and designers to produce a single book. In the digital world, the role of publishers will be larger as new technologies provide for an even greater user and learning experience. Furthermore, with the skyrocketing amount of content being served on the web, customers will seek and pay expert content providers that aggregate and contextualize information for them efficiently and provide highly accurate and specific search options. Publishers with expertise and resources in these and emerging areas will be the ones that write the new rules of e-book publishing.

E-books Will Change the Textbook Business

Jeffrey R. Young

Jeffrey R. Young is a senior writer for The Chronicle of Higher Education, *a newspaper and website that provides news and information for college and university faculty members, administrators, and students. College 2.0 covers how new technologies are changing colleges. Please send ideas to jeff.young@ chronicle.com or @jryoung on Twitter.*

Y ou've heard it before: Digital technologies blew up the music industry's moneymaking model, and the textbook business is next.

For years observers have predicted a coming wave of e-textbooks. But so far it just hasn't happened. One explanation for the delay is that while music fans were eager to try a new, more portable form of entertainment, students tend to be more conservative when choosing required materials for their studies. For a real disruption in the textbook market, students may have to be forced to change.

That's exactly what some companies and college leaders are now proposing. They're saying that e-textbooks should be required reading and that colleges should be the ones charging for them. It is the best way to control skyrocketing costs and may actually save the textbook industry from digital piracy, they claim. Major players like the McGraw-Hill Companies, Pearson, and John Wiley & Sons are getting involved.

To understand what a radical shift that would be, think about the current textbook model. Every professor expects students to have ready access to required texts, but technically, purchasing them is optional. So over the years students have improvised a range of ways to dodge buying a new copy—picking up a used textbook, borrowing a copy from the library, sharing with a roommate, renting one, downloading an illegal version, or simply going without. Publishers collect a fee only when students buy new books, giving the companies a financial impetus to crank out updated editions whether the content needs refreshing or not.

Here's the new plan: Colleges require students to pay a course-materials fee, which would be used to buy e-books for all of them (whatever text the professor recommends, just as in the old model).

Why electronic copies? Well, they're far cheaper to produce than printed texts, making a bulk purchase more feasible. By ordering books by the hundreds or thousands, colleges can negotiate a much better rate than students were able to get on their own, even for used books. And publishers could eliminate the used-book market and reduce incentives for students to illegally download copies as well.

The real champions of the change are the college officials signing the deals.

Of course those who wanted to read the textbook on paper could print out the electronic version or pay an additional fee to buy an old-fashioned copy—a book.

Some for-profit colleges, including the University of Phoenix, already do something like this, but the practice has been rare on traditional campuses.

An Indiana company called Courseload hopes to make the model more widespread, by serving as a broker for colleges willing to impose the requirement on students. And it is not alone. The upstart publisher Flat World Knowledge recently made a bulk deal with Virginia State University's business school, and last month the company hired a new salesperson devoted entirely to "institutional sales" of its e-textbooks. And Daytona State College, in Florida, is negotiating with publishers to test a similar arrangement.

The real champions of the change are the college officials signing the deals. They say they felt compelled to act after seeing students drop out because they could not afford textbooks, whose average prices rose 186 percent between 1986 and 2005, and continue to shoot up each year far faster than inflation.

"When students pay more for new textbooks than tuition in a year, then something's wrong," says Rand S. Spiwak, executive vice president at Daytona State, who is leading the experiment there. "Our game plan is to bring the cost of textbooks down by 75 to 80 percent."

Apple reset the sales model for music, with its iPod players and market-leading online store, and the company is likely to try to enter the e-textbook market as well. But watch out, publishers, the change agents for textbooks may just be traditional colleges.

Courseload's system . . . brings in content from various publishers and allows annotation and other features.

Moving the Tollbooth

Courseload, the e-book broker, started in 2000, when a cofounder, Mickey Levitan, a former Apple employee inspired by the company's transformative role in the music industry, devised the idea and teamed up with a professor at Indiana University at Bloomington to try it. But the company failed to find enough takers, and it all but shut down after a brief run.

Then last year an official at Indiana, Bradley C. Wheeler, called Mr. Levitan and talked him into trying again.

Mr. Wheeler is part of an effort at the university to bring down textbook costs, and he remembered a conversation he had had with Mr. Levitan about the idea 10 years ago. Back then, Mr. Wheeler was just a professor of business, but now he is also vice president for information technology and able to help try the approach, which he calls "moving the toll-booth" for textbooks.

"Universities are going to have to engage in saying, 'This is how we want e-textbook models to evolve that are advantageous to our students and our interests,'" he told me this month.

For three semesters Indiana has tested Courseload's system, which brings in content from various publishers and allows annotation and other features. So far the company has persuaded McGraw-Hill, Pearson, and John Wiley to participate. During those first experiments, students were not charged, and the university and Courseload paid for the e-textbooks. But Mr. Wheeler said that in the spring the university would try at least one pilot where students would pay a mandatory fee for the e-textbooks, which he expected to be about $35 per course in most cases.

Company and university officials gingerly approached two key groups early on: students and state legislators. Mr. Wheeler said student-government officials he talked to were supportive. Mr. Levitan said that the legislators generally opposed new fees, but sympathized with the project's goal of reducing overall costs to students and said they would not oppose it.

Mr. Levitan said the company was running tests at a handful of colleges, though he declined to name them.

The Virginia Pilot

Mirta Martin, dean of Virginia State's business school, speaks passionately about her reasons for taking part in the experiment with Flat World, which makes e-textbooks standard in eight courses this fall.

"For our accounting books senior year, there's nothing under $250," she told me this summer. "What the students were saying is, We don't have the money to purchase these books."

Last year Ms. Martin became so frustrated over hearing stories about students who were performing poorly because they could not afford textbooks that she pledged that no needy student would go without a book. At first she asked community leaders and others to donate to a fund to pay for the books of students who sought financial help. Last year that project bought $4,000 worth of books for students.

But Ms. Martin felt that the philanthropic model was not sustainable, so she began reaching out to publishers to see if the institution could get some sort of bulk rate that would allow it to pay for textbooks for all students.

In its standard model, Flat World offers free access to its textbooks while students are online. If students want to download a copy to their own computers, they must pay $24.95 for a PDF (a print edition costs about $30). But the publisher offered the Virginia State business school a bulk rate of $20 per student per course, and it will allow students at the school to download not only the digital copies but also the study guide, an audio version, or an iPad edition (a bundle that would typically cost about $100).

Tricky issues remain, though. What if a professor wrote the textbook assigned for his or her class? Is it ethical to force students to buy it, even at a reduced rate? And what if students feel they are better off on their own, where they have the option of sharing or borrowing a book at no cost?

Proponents of the new model argue that in time policies can be developed and prices can be driven low enough to win widespread support.

If so, more changes are bound to follow. In music, the Internet reduced album sales as more people bought only the individual songs they wanted. For textbooks, that may mean letting students (or brokers at colleges) buy only the chapters they want. Or only supplementary materials like instructional videos and interactive homework problems, all delivered on-line.

And that really would be the end of the textbook as we know it.

E-books May Result in the End of Libraries as Book-Lending Institutions

Jonathan Rochkind

Jonathan Rochkind is a systems librarian and a blogger at Bibliographic Wilderness, a blog about library matters such as digital systems and services, metadata, cataloging, and methods for navigating the information world.

Why a shift to ebooks imperils libraries: It isn't because libraries can't figure out, technically, how to loan out ebooks. It's because publishers don't *want* them to, and may be able to prevent it.

The Threat to Libraries

A shift to ebooks has been predicted for a while, and seems to be happening. I've talked to many people who wonder why their public libraries don't offer more ebooks they can download on their e-reader of choice, assuming it's because the public libraries don't want to, or are not technically competent to. The first is, I think, definitely no longer true—libraries want to. The second, technical competence, may be a barrier, but it's not the prime one.

The prime barrier is that publishers by and large don't *want* libraries to. I don't think most library patrons realize the threat to libraries here—I think it's high-time library organizations like the ALA [American Library Association] start educating them. Most people like public libraries and want them to continue; a public that realizes they may be threatened will be more likely to support policy to make them do so, and that's what's needed.

[There are] difficulties in running a kindle lending program.

With a print book, a library can buy a book and loan it to as many borrowers as they like, without any permission from the publisher at all. In the US, the right to do this is protected by the first sale doctrine.

That does not apply to ebooks. I do not have the right to buy an ebook and loan it out again. I need the publisher's permission—I may also need enabling technology to make it possible, vs Digital Rights Management [DRM] that actively seeks to prevent it (and the DMCA [Digital Millennium Copyright Act] which makes it illegal to violate that DRM technology). A publisher can charge dearly for that permission, or withhold it entirely. With a print book, a publisher might still be worried that being able to borrow for free from a library can hurt sales—but they can't do anything about it. With an ebook, they can do something about it, the balance of powers has shifted tectonically in favor of publishers. . . .

Difficulties in Lending E-books

Patrick Berry of California State University Chico [has commented] on the difficulties in running a kindle lending program. Patrick investigates the feasibility of loaning out actual physical kindles loaded with titles purchased by the library—this used to be somewhat feasible, but recently Amazon made technical changes that require a purchased title to be registered to a *particular* kindle device when purchased, and only readable on that device. Actually, to be fair, Amazon allows up to *six* devices to be registered for a title. But if a library wants to purchase more than six physical kindle devices, then a given title they purchase they can only load on six of them, unless they buy multiple copies. Note that this isn't only six *at once*, it's only six specific physical devices, pretty much ever.

What if you instead of loaning out actual physical kindles, a library wanted to loan out kindle titles for patrons to load on their own kindles? Well, that same restriction makes it impossible for a library to simply buy the book normally at a normal rate and loan it out themselves directly to patrons (as libraries do with print books).

Now, you may have heard that Amazon recently announced a program with Overdrive to support library lending. The details of this program are vague and don't seem available on the open internet. It seems likely to me that not *every* title available for kindle is in the Overdrive library program, probably only titles that publishers opted in to. (Compare to ordinary print books, where a library can buy any book at all and lend it out). Likewise, it seems likely that libraries *pay* more over the lifetime of use for a kindle Overdrive title than they would for a print title. I don't know what the library pricing model is here, and would be very very curious if anyone does—does a library pay an up front 'purchase' fee, is it more than the usual kindle purchase fee? Does the library pay a per-checkout fee as well? (something a library does *not* do with a print book, and there'd be no way for a publisher to require it).

Libraries can offer ebooks, unlike print books, only at the sufferance of publishers, and publishers may charge whatever they like for this 'privilege'. Publishers, not liking the idea of libraries much, are not providing that permission in some cases, and are providing pricing models in other cases which make it much more expensive for a library to offer an ebook than a print book. If reader preferences continue to shift to ebooks as we expect, we may very well see the end of libraries as book lending institutions. *Not* because patrons don't want to borrow ebooks from a library same as they did print ebooks, *not* because libraries don't want to loan ebooks or can't figure out the technology, *but* because publishers simply don't want it to happen, and our laws give them the right to prevent it.

Organizations to Contact

The editors have compiled the following list of organizations concerned with the issues debated in this book. The descriptions are derived from materials provided by the organizations. All have publications or information available for interested readers. The list was compiled on the date of publication of the present volume; the information provided here may change. Be aware that many organizations take several weeks or longer to respond to inquiries, so allow as much time as possible.

American Library Association (ALA)

50 E Huron St., Chicago, IL   60611
(800) 545-2433 • fax: (312) 440-9374
e-mail: ala@ala.org
website: www.ala.org

The American Library Association was founded in 1876 to help develop and promote libraries in the United States in order to enhance learning and ensure access to information for all. The ALA publishes a number of periodicals, including *American Libraries, Booklist,* and *Library Technology Reports,* and a search of the ALA website for e-book produces a list of publications related to this subject.

Association of American Publishers (AAP)

455 Massachusetts Ave. NW, Suite 700
Washington, DC   20001-2777
(202) 347-3375 • fax: (202) 347-3690
e-mail: info@publishers.org
website: www.publishers.org

The Association of American Publishers is a trade association for US book publishers. It represents the industry's interests on policy, legislative, and regulatory issues regionally, nationally, and worldwide. These interests include the protection of intellectual property rights and worldwide copyright enforcement, digital and new technology issues, funding for education and libraries, tax and trade, censorship, and literacy. Resources available on the AAP website include the following reports: *E-reader Ownership Doubles in Six Months*, *Tablet Adoption Grows More Slowly*, and *One in Six Americans Now Use E-Reader with One in Six Likely to Purchase in Next Six Months*.

Google Books

1600 Amphitheatre Pkwy., Mountain View, CA   94043
website: http://books.google.com

Google Books, one part of Google, Inc., searches the full text of books that Google has scanned, converted to text, and stored in digital form. Subscribers to the service can download books that are in the public domain, view pages from books that are out of copyright (or from those for which copyright owners have given permission), and view certain pages or parts of in-print books that are protected by copyright. Google is also partnering with some libraries and publishers to scan additional copyrighted books and make them available to subscribers.

Independent Book Publishers Association (IBPA)

1020 Manhattan Beach Blvd., Suite 204
Manhattan Beach, CA   90266
(310) 546-1818 • fax: (310) 546-3939
e-mail: info@IBPA-online.org
website: www.ibpa-online.org

The Independent Book Publishers Association is a nonprofit trade association representing independent book publishers in the United States and elsewhere around the world. It seeks to advance the professional interests of independent publishers by providing cooperative marketing programs, education, and advocacy within the publishing industry. The IBPA website is a source of articles about publishing, including e-book publishing. Examples include: "Save Time and Money by Designing with E-books in Mind," "E-book Conversions: Ten Pointers to Ensure Reader Enjoyment (and Minimize E-book Returns)," and "E-book Reality Show (and Tell)."

Novelists, Inc. (Ninc)
PO Box 2037, Manhattan, KS 66505
fax: (785) 537-1877
e-mail: ninc@varney.com
website: www.ninc.com

Novelists, Inc. promotes the creative contributions of novelists and their rights to be treated with dignity, to be recognized as the sole owners of their literary creations, and to be fairly compensated for their writings. Ninc publishes a blog, a newsletter, and various other booklets, including two relating to digital publishing: *A Comprehensive Guide to the New World of Publishing* and *The Future of Publishing.*

Pew Internet & American Life Project
1615 L St. NW, Suite 700, Washington, DC 20036
(202) 419-4300 • fax: (202) 419-4349
website: www.pewinternet.org

The Pew Internet & American Life Project is one of seven projects that make up the Pew Research Center, a nonpartisan, nonprofit "fact tank" that provides information on the issues, attitudes, and trends shaping life in the United States and other countries around the world. The Project produces reports exploring the impact of the Internet and digital media on families, communities, work and home, daily life, education, health care, and civic and political life. The website links users to publications on e-books such as *Tablet and E-book Reader Ownership Nearly Double Over the Holiday Gift-Giving Period* and *E-reader Ownership Doubles in Six Months.*

Project Gutenberg Literary Archive Foundation (PGLAF)
809 N 1500 W, Salt Lake City, UT 84116
e-mail: help2010@pglaf.org
website: www.gutenberg.org

Project Gutenberg is a collection of free electronic books, or e-books, founded by Michael Hart, the inventor of e-books. The project's mission is to encourage the creation and distribution of e-books and help give them away. The website has a search engine that offers various ways to browse and select free e-books.

Bibliography

Books

Robert Darnton — *The Case for Books: Past, Present, and Future*. New York: PublicAffairs, 2009.

Kathleen Fitzpatrick — *Planned Obsolescence: Publishing, Technology, and the Future of the Academy*. New York: New York University Press, 2011.

Oliver A. Hagen, ed. — *Digital Books: Competition and Commerce*. Hauppauge, NY: Nova Science, 2010.

Linda Houle — *The Naked Truth About Book Publishing*. Spring, TX: Wisdom Trends, 2010.

Ioannis Iglezakis, Tatiana-Eleni Synodinou, and Sarantos Kapidakis — *E-Publishing and Digital Libraries: Legal and Organizational Issues*. Hershey, PA: IGI Global, 2010.

Bill Kovarik — *Revolutions in Communication: Media History from Gutenberg to the Digital Age*. New York: Continuum International, 2011.

J. Steve Miller et al. — *Sell More Books! Book Marketing and Publishing for Low Profile and Debut Authors Rethinking Book Publicity after the Digital Revolutions*. Acworth, GA: Wisdom Creek Press, 2011.

Ksenija
Mincic-Obradovic

E-books in Academic Libraries.
Oxford, United Kingdom: Chandos,
2010.

Gail M. Nelson

*E-Books Simplified: The Step-by-Step
Guide to E-Publishing.* Charleston,
SC: CreateSpace, 2011.

Sue Polanka, ed.

*No Shelf Required 2: Use and
Management of Electronic Books.*
Chicago, IL: American Library
Association Editions, 2012.

Kate Price and
Virginia Havergal

*E-books in Libraries: A Practical
Guide.* London, United Kingdom:
Facet, 2011.

Carolyn P.
Schriber

*The Second Mouse Gets the Cheese:
How to Avoid the Traps of
Self-Publishing.* Cordova, TN:
Katzenhaus Books, 2012.

Sally Shields,
Gang Chen, et al.

*Outskirts Press Presents the Highly
Effective Habits of 5 Successful
Authors: How They Beat the
Self-Publishing Odds, and How You
Can, Too.* Parker, CO: Outskirts
Press, 2010.

Karin Wikoff

*Electronic Resources Management in
the Academic Library: A Professional
Guide.* Santa Barbara, CA: Libraries
Unlimited/ABC-CLIO, 2011.

John Willinsky

*The Access Principle: The Case for
Open Access to Research and
Scholarship.* Cambridge, MA: MIT
Press, 2006.

Periodicals and Internet Sources

al.com

"A House Divided: The E-book Debate Hits Home," February 12, 2012. www.al.com.

Julie Bosman

"Publisher Limits Shelf Life for Library E-books," *New York Times*, March 14, 2011. www.nytimes.com.

Julie Bosman and Edward Wyatt

"Who Should Control E-book Pricing? Publishers, Apple Accused of Conspiring to Keep Prices Higher," *Columbus Dispatch*, March 12, 2012. www.dispatch.com.

Roger Brisson

"The E-book Debate," The Personal Website of Roger Brisson. www.humanismus.com.

Janice D'Arcy

"Are Electronic Children's Books as Good as 'Old-School' Books?" *Washington Post*, December 20, 2011. www.washingtonpost.com.

Rebekah Denn

"Limits on Library E-books Stir Controversy," *Christian Science Monitor*, February 28, 2011. www.csmonitor.com.

Mathew Ingram

"DOJ Warning Means One Thing: E-book Prices Are Coming Down," BloombergBusinessweek, March 9, 2012. www.businessweek.com.

Hannah Johnson   "#BEA11: Publishers Debate Future of Enhanced E-books at IDPF Conference," Publishing Perspectives, May 23, 2011. http://publishing perspectives.com.

Hannah Johnson   "California Librarian Calls for E-book Lending Action," Publishing Perspectives, February 10, 2012. http://publishingperspectives.com.

Carolyn Kellogg   "Digital Book World: Where Do Libraries and E-books Meet?" *Los Angeles Times*, January 26, 2011. http://latimesblogs.latimes.com.

Library Renewal   "$2 Billion for $1 Billion of Books: The Arithmetic of Library E-book Lending," March 5, 2012. http://libraryrenewal.org.

Joel Mathis and Ben Boychuk   "Debate: E-books and the Future of Democracy," *Newsday*, February 2, 2012. www.newsday.com.

Kristen Mitchell and Kaitor Kposowa   "Will E-books Replace College Textbooks?" *The Lantern*, February 15, 2012. www.thelantern.com.

Lynn Neary   "The Future of Libraries in the E-book Age," *All Things Considered*, April 4, 2011. www.npr.org.

New York Times   "Does the Brain Like E-books?" October 14, 2009. http://roomfor debate.blogs.nytimes.com.

Ed Pilkington   "Amanda Hocking, the Writer Who Made Millions by Self-Publishing Online," *Guardian*, January 12, 2012. www.guardian.co.uk.

Christopher Platt   "The Happy Reader Equation: A Librarian on HarperCollins's E-book Pricing Model," *Publishers Weekly*, March 14, 2011. www.publishers weekly.com.

Brad Stone   "Amazon's Hit Man," BloombergBusinessweek, January 25, 2012. www.businessweek.com.

David Streitfeld   "Amazon Signs Up Authors, Writing Publishers Out of Deal," *New York Times*, October 16, 2011. www.ny times.com.

Susannah Tredwell   "The Use of E-Books in Law Libraries: Legal Libraries Face Special Challenges in Adopting E-books, but the Pressures to Do So Will Only Grow Greater Over Time," *Information Outlook*, July 1, 2011. www.thefreelibrary.com.

Index

A

ACS4 format for e-books, 22
Adobe Content Server 4, 22
Adobe Digital Editions (ADE), 30, 57, 66
Adobe ePub, 22, 57
Adobe PDF formatting
  e-publishing and, 33
  for libraries, 29
  popularity of, 15–16
  public domain books in, 22
Agency pricing model
  by Amazon, 91
  by Apple, 79, 84, 95, 96
  publisher embrace of, 80
  wholesale pricing model *vs.*, 96–98
Amazon
  e-book lending library, 46–47
  e-book prices, 78–79, 81–82, 83–86, 128
  as e-book publisher, 64, 85
  e-book publishing through, 32–33
  e-book sales, 16, 18, 78, 85, 121
  Kindle 2, 23–24
  Kindle DX, 23
  Kindle Fire, 19, 85
  Kindle Touch, 18
  library competition with, 56
  library support for, 87–88
  Overdrive program and, 138
  predatory pricing by, 62, 96–98
  self-publishing with, 94–95, 105, 121

  terms for publishers, 91–92
  See also Kindle
Amazon Prime Service, 46
American Library Association (ALA), 46, 63, 68, 74, 136
Anderson, Kent, 62–64
Android devices, 20, 57, 127
Android Media Console, 57
Apple
  agency pricing model by, 79, 84, 95, 96
  digital music sales, 82, 132
  e-book pricing, 79–80, 98
  e-book sales, 18, 78
  iBooks, 20, 101
  iPad 2, 19
  iPod, 132
  price colluding investigation of, 80, 96, 99
  price control by, 93
  as publisher, 64
  textbook program by, 63
  See also iPad
Applebaum, Stuart, 73–74, 76
Aquinas, Thomas, 14
Association of American Publishers, 121
AT&T wireless, 19
Austen, Jane, 119
Authors Guild, 96, 97, 99, 101
AZW file format, 22, 29

B

Baker, Dean, 100
Barnes & Noble
  e-book lending library, 46

e-book sales, 18, 121
library competition with, 56
Nook Simple Touch, 18, 19
See also Nook Tablet
BBeB file format, 22
Blackberry devices, 20
Blessings (Quindlen), 72
BlueFire client software, 57
Borders book stores, 22
Brewer, Carolyn, 75
Brown University, 14
Busa, Roberto, 14

C

Cellular wireless network, 19
Center for Economic and Policy
  Research, 100
Chan, Darcie, 124
Chief Officers of State Library
  Agencies (COSLA), 26
Cleantech, 42
Cloud technology, 20
Collins, Suzanne, 102
Cooper, Charles, 83–86
Copyright issues, 22, 137
Courseload (e-book broker), 131,
  132–133
Cross, Jason, 21–25

D

Dayton Metro Libraries, 30–31
Daytona State College, 132
Didion, Joan, 109
Digital divide, 38–40
Digital Millennium Copyright Act
  (DMCA), 137
Digital music sales, 82

Digital rights management (DRM)
  e-book pricing and, 81
  for e-readers, 39
  in library e-books, 27, 53, 137
  varying support for, 21–22
Donahue, Deirdre, 120–125
Douglas County Libraries, 30–31
Downloading e-book content,
  29–30
Dylan, Bob, 40

E

E-books
  advantages of, 21–25
  allow self-publishing, 32–33
  benefits of, 26–31
  demand for, 14, 65–66
  digital divide concerns with,
    38–40
  free content with, 28
  future of, 21–22
  green rating for, 41–43
  industry changes, 70–71
  lending difficulties, 45–46,
    137–139
  lending technology, 35, 38–39
  overview, 14–16, 18–20
E-books, future
  contextual upsell with, 128
  decline of print journalism,
    108–111
  digital content of, 107–113
  five trends in, 126–129
  overview, 105–106
  paper books *vs.*, 114–119
  potential of, 118–119
  publisher importance, 128–
    129
  self-publishing and, 32–33,
    120–125

steppingstones to success, 124–125
success of, 121–122
textbook business and, 130–135
threat to libraries, 136–139
video in, 126
writing and technology, 117–118
E-books, pricing
consumer impact, 94
costs must cover publishing, 89–91
as e-book publisher decision, 81–82
fairness of, 100–101
lawsuit impact on, 99–103
losses from, 93–95
overview, 77–80
war over, 81–82
E-books, publishers/publishing
Amazon as, 64, 85
Amazon terms for, 91–92
costs must cover, 89–91
e-book pricing decisions, 81–82
e-readers and, 32–33
lending restrictions by, 138–139
library sales by, 45
loss of sales from high prices, 16, 78, 93–95
new rules for, 129
useable formats for, 15
Editing
in college writing, 117
costs, 78, 88, 90
illegal pirating of, 125
need for, 33, 64, 90
by publishers, 102
E-ink reader technology, 18, 23–24

Eisenhower in War and Peace (Smith), 72
Electronic Publication (EPUB), 15
The End of Faith (Harris), 108
ePub books. See Adobe ePub
E-readers
benefits of, 36–37
need for, 39–40
publishing and, 32–33
technology differences among, 70
text-to-speech features, 81
types of, 22–25
See also iPad; Kindle; Nook Tablet; Sony readers
European Union (EU), 84

F

Facebook, 57, 59, 105, 109–110
Fall of Giants (Follett), 93
Ferriss, Tim, 85, 110
Filloux, Frederic, 97–98
Film industry comparisons, 50, 114, 115
First-sale doctrine, 45, 60
Fisher-Herreman, Scarlett, 74–75
Flat World Knowledge, 131–132, 133
Follett, Ken, 93
Font size adjustments, 21
Free Press publishing, 112
Freethy, Barbara, 122
FRESS system, 15

G

Galaxy Tab, 127
Garcia, Trent, 75
Godin, Seth, 110

Gonzales, Guy LeCharles, 67
Google (search engine), 16, 56
Google Books, 16, 63
Google Play, 79
Guardian (newspaper), 97
Gutenberg, Johannes, 15, 125

H

Hachette Book Group
  library sales by, 27, 45, 65
  price colluding investigation
    of, 80, 96, 99
  value of e-books, 94
Haq, Husna, 96–98
HarperCollins
  boycott of, 59–61
  e-book rental limitations, 45–
    46, 65, 70–71
  price colluding investigation
    of, 80, 96, 99
Harris, Sam, 107–113
Hart, Michael S., 15
High-definition television, 115–
  116
Hitchens, Christopher, 108–110
Hocking, Amanda, 94, 105–106,
  124–125
HTML code, 33
Hunger Games (Collins), 102

I

iBooks (Apple), 20, 101
iLex reader, 127
Independent Publishers Group
  (IPG), 67, 79, 83, 87–88
Indiana University, 132
Ingram, Mathew, 93–95

Intellectual property (IP) owners,
  55
Interead Cool-ER, 24–25
International Digital Publishing
  Forum (IDPF), 15
iPad (Apple)
  consumer confusion over, 127
  e-book lending library, 46
  e-book pricing, 83–84
  e-books on, 14
  format of, 16
  impact on reading, 119
  Kindle reader for, 101
  library patrons and, 27
  popularity of, 19, 41, 94
  self-published e-books on,
    105, 121
iPad 2 (Apple), 19
iPad 3 (Apple), 99
iPod (Apple), 132
Isaacson, Walter, 84

J

Jobs, Steve, 79, 83–84
John Wiley & Sons publishing,
  130, 133
Joyce, James, 119

K

Kambitsch, Tim, 53–58
Keillor, Garrison, 118–119
Kelley, Michael, 72–76
Keyboard technology, 23
Kindle (Amazon)
  AZW file format, 22, 29
  consumer confusion over,
    127–128
  e-books on, 14
  format of, 16, 20, 22, 35

impact on reading, 119
for libraries, 27, 38
popularity of, 34, 41, 94, 101,
  128
self-publishing and, 33, 121
wireless-transfer convenience,
  21
Kindle 2, 23–24
Kindle DX, 23
Kindle Fire (Amazon), 19, 85
Kindle Touch (Amazon), 18
Konrath, J. A., 106, 123

L

LaRue, Jamie, 31
LCD screen technology, 19
Leibovitz, Annie, 109
Lending technology
  difficulty with, 45–46, 137–
    139
  of e-books, 35, 38–39
  restrictions by publishers,
    138–139
Levitan, Mickey, 132–133
Libraries
  Amazon support by, 87–88
  downloading e-book content,
    29–30
  e-book lending difficulties,
    45–46, 137–139
  e-book threat to, 136–139
  ePub books for, 22
  Kindle-compatible e-books in,
    38
  patron needs, 27–28
Libraries, should buy e-books
  benefits, 26–31
  cost concerns, 31, 53–55
  free e-book content availabil-
    ity, 28

future concerns, 57–58
hosting options, 55–56
need for, 26–27, 53–58
open environment needs,
  53–55
overview, 45–47
paid rental option, 51
price-point concerns, 50–52
public demand over, 62–64
rental market needed, 48–52
sellers and concerns over,
  59–61
staff training needs, 30–31
Libraries, should not buy e-books
  cost concerns, 27, 72–76
  frustration over, 74–76
  patron needs, 65–68
  reasons for, 69–71
  solution needed over, 67–68
Library Journal (magazine), 73
Lincoln, Abraham, 39–40
Locke, John, 94
Lyons, C. J., 125

M

Mac computers, 20
Macmillan publishing
  Amazon pricing war, 79–82
  library sales by, 27, 45, 49, 63
  price colluding investigation
    of, 80, 96, 99
Mallory, H. P., 106
Manjoo, Farhad, 101–102
MARC (Machine- Readable
  Cataloging), 29
Martin, Andrew, 125
Martin, Mirta, 133–134
Matthews, Curt, 87–88, 89–91
McGraw-Hill, 126, 129, 130, 133
McLuhan, Marshall, 114–116, 119

The Mill River (Chan), 124
Millsap, Gina, 74–75
Mims, Christopher, 38–40
Minotaur Press, 125
Movable type, 114
MP3 players, 23, 25

N

New York Public Library, 74
New York Times (newspaper), 42, 111
The New Yorker (magazine), 108
Newbie's Guide to Publishing (website), 123
Newman, Bobbi, 65–68
Nook Simple Touch (Barnes & Noble), 18, 19
Nook Tablet (Barnes & Noble)
    consumer confusion over, 127
    format of, 20, 35
    library patrons and, 27
    overview, 19
    popularity of, 34
    self-published e-books on, 105, 121
North Texas Library Partners, 75

O

Oberhausen, Debbie, 72
OPAC (online public access catalog), 29
Open e-Book Publication Structure (OEBPS), 15
Oprah Press, 102
Overdrive hosting
    Amazon program with, 138
    e-book costs, 72, 74–75
    ePub-formatted books by, 57

    HarperCollins relationship with, 59
    Kindle downloads by, 29
    as library supplier, 27, 54, 55, 61, 121
    tech support from, 70

P

Paid rental option, 51
PC computers, 20, 23, 27, 117–118
PDF formating. *See* Adobe PDF formatting
Pearson publishing, 130, 133
Penguin Group
    library sales by, 27, 45, 63, 65
    price colluding investigation of, 80, 96, 99
Perenson, Melissa J., 21–25
Petlewski, Kathy, 75–76
Pew Internet & American Life Project, 26–27
Platt, Christopher, 74
Plymouth District Library, 75
Polanka, Sue, 26–31
Potzsch, Oliver, 106
Prescott, Michael, 120–122
Printed (paper) books
    advantages of, 34–37
    cost of, 89–90
    decline of, 108–111
    e-books *vs.*, 114–119
    future difficulties for, 111–113
    as greener than e-books, 41–43
Project Gutenberg, 15
Public domain books, 22
PublicLibraries.com, 87–88
Publishing (publishers), 126–129

See also E-books, publishers/
publishing; Self-publishing;
individual publishers

Q

Quindlen, Anna, 72

R

Ramos, Bethany, 32–33
Random House publishing, 27, 46,
65, 72–76
Ratcliff, Trey, 64
Riptide (Prescott), 120
Rochkind, Jonathan, 136–139
RocketBook device, 126
RosettaBooks, 85
Royalty rates, 87, 89, 91
Ruppel, Philip, 126–129

S

Sammons, Eric, 34–37
San Francisco Public Library, 75
Sargent, John, 49
Schneider, Karen, 67–68
Schulman, Janet, 75
Scilken, Marvin, 68
A Secret Wish (Freethy), 122
Self-publishing
with Amazon, 94–95
e-books allow, 32–33, 120–125
popularity of, 105–106
The Shadow Hunter (Prescott), 122
Shanley, Lorraine, 94
Sheehan, Kate, 59–61
Shipping costs, 91
Sierra Club Green Home, 41–43,
42

Sierra Magazine, 41
Simon & Schuster
library sales by, 27, 45, 63, 65
price colluding investigation
of, 80, 96, 99
Smartphones, 27, 29, 121
Smith, Jean Edward, 72
Social networking sites, 19, 57
See also Facebook; Twitter
Sony Reader Pocket, 24
Sony Reader Touch, 22–23
Sony readers
BBeB file format of, 22
consumer confusion over, 127
self-published e-books on,
105, 121
Spellman, John, 85
Spiwak, Rand S., 132
Sprint wireless, 23
St. Martin's Press, 106, 124, 125
Stylus technology, 22
Swafford, Jan, 114–119

T

3G/4G service, 19, 23
Tablets
e-book prices for, 78
as e-readers, 39
Kindle 2, 23–24
Kindle Fire, 19, 85
overview, 18–20
popularity of, 27, 66
reading applications for,
29–30
See also iPad; individual tab-
lets
Taylor, Martin, 48–52
Technology and writing, 117–118
Telegraph, 115
Television (TV), 115–116

The 10 Easter Egg Hunters (Schulman), 75
TendersInfo News, 81–82
TerraPass study, 42
Textbook business
    by Apple, 63
    e-book changes to, 130–135
    overview, 130–131
Text-to-speech features, 81
Topeka and Shawnee County Public Library, 74
Touchscreens, 18, 19, 22
Turow, Scott, 96–98, 99–102
Twitter, 57, 59, 105, 109–110

U

United Kingdom (UK), 48–50
University of Illinois, 15
University of Phoenix, 131
US Declaration of Independence, 15
US Justice Department (DOJ) lawsuit, 79–80, 84, 96, 98–103
USA Today (newspaper), 120, 122, 124
USB cables, 24, 30

V

Van Dam, Andries, 14–15
Vanity Fair (magazine), 109–110

Video in e-books, 126
Virginia State University, 131–133
Vision-impaired benefits of e-books, 21

W

Wall Street Journal (newspaper), 93–95
Warehousing costs, 91
Washington Post (newspaper), 62–63
Wheeler, Bradley C., 132–133
Wholesale pricing model, 78, 79, 91, 96–98
Wi-Fi accessibility, 19
Williamson, Evan, 69–71
Winfrey, Oprah, 102
Wireless-transfer convenience, 21, 24–25
Writing and technology, 117–118

Y

The Year of Magical Thinking (Didion), 109
Yeats, William Butler, 119
Yglesias, Matthew, 99–103
Young, Jeffrey R., 130–135
YouTube, 30, 111